Dr Grahame Howard was born in London in 1953 and his family moved to Norwich when he was four years old. His childhood, particularly the eccentric behaviour of his father, is documented in his first book, 'The Tales of Dod', published in 2010. He returned to London to study Medicine at St Thomas' Hospital Medical School, from where he graduated in 1976. Following a series of junior doctor posts in both London and Cambridge he was appointed consultant Clinical Oncologist in Edinburgh in 1986. His subsequent career was spent at the Edinburgh Western General Hospital, specialising in prostate and testicular cancer, eventually becoming Clinical Director of the Edinburgh Cancer Centre, an examiner for the Royal College of Radiologists and assistant editor of Clinical Oncology. 'Spoz and his Friends' documents the writer's life as a medical student in the 1970s, and relates with humour the faltering transition of these young men from schoolboys to newly-qualified doctors.

Spoz and friends: Tales of a London medical student

To Richard, Michael and Charles.

Grahame C. W. Howard

SPOZ AND FRIENDS: TALES OF A LONDON MEDICAL STUDENT

AUSTIN MACAULEY
PUBLISHERS LTD.

A CIP catalogue record for this title is available from the British Library.

ISBN 978 1 84963 204 8

www.austinmacauley.com

First Published (2013)
Austin Macauley Publishers Ltd.
25 Canada Square
Canary Wharf
London
E14 5LB

Printed & Bound in Great Britain

With grateful thanks to the staff and patients of St Thomas' Hospital Medical School.

Contents

Chapter 1: Spoz Leaves Home 17

Chapter 2: Skeletons And Cadavers 29

Chapter 3: Law And Disorder 41

Chapter 4: Myopia And A Mismatch 52

Chapter 5: The Glass Eye And The Mortuary Trolley 61

Chapter 6: Down And Out In Clapham And Brixton 75

Chapter 7: Short White Coats 87

Chapter 8: Pubar 97

Chapter 9: Onwards And Upwards 112

Chapter 10: The Klokowox 125

Chapter 11: Pay-Day Philosophy 135

Chapter 12: The Clavicle Club 151

Chapter 13: A Little Unpleasantness At Gassiott House 167

Chapter 14: Sojourn In Soho: And The Price Of Sex 179

Chapter 15: Having A Ball 191

Chapter 16: The End Of An Era 202

'Would I were in an alehouse in London! I would give all my fame for a pot of ale and safety.'

Shakespeare. Henry V Act 3

CHAPTER 1:

SPOZ LEAVES HOME

It was twenty minutes past ten on a pleasant, balmy, sunny morning in early autumn; the kind of day when London is at its best, with the capital's trees just beginning their annual transformation from drab summer green into the glorious, vibrant reds and browns of autumn. As I'd walked along the Embankment to St Thomas' Hospital the view across the Thames to the Houses of Parliament had been uplifting and my spirits were high. Now, my exuberance had evaporated and I was gripped by an overwhelming anxiety as I waited, alone and nervous, outside the Nevin lecture theatre on my first day as a medical student.

The institution that would attempt to transform me from errant schoolboy to respected doctor was St Thomas' Hospital Medical School, arguably the oldest in London. This hospital was already considered ancient in 1215, when it was run by a mixed order of Augustinian monks and nuns dedicated to Thomas à Becket. Then it had been located in Southwark, ministering to the poor, the sick and the homeless of that dockland borough. King Henry VIII disapproved of it, considering it to be a 'bawdy house' – probably because it treated prostitutes – and had it dissolved in 1510, only for it to be opened again after some forty years, re-dedicated to St Thomas the Apostle. It was Florence Nightingale, three hundred years later, who advised that the hospital should move to its current site on the east bank of the Thames, opposite the Houses of Parliament. In 1862 this grand Victorian edifice opened its doors to the sick and the lame of Lambeth, and in 1970 opened them to me.

I was called the 'Spoz' – not my real name of course, but one given me about ten years earlier by my elder brother, the 'Woog'. I had just turned seventeen, and was six foot four, gawky and shy, with long curly hair and a prominent nose. My main talent lay in drinking beer, a skill I had inherited from my father, who was known to the family as 'the Dod'. I could drink a pint in five seconds and remain standing when most of my friends had been rendered unconscious; and I also played the piano. On this glorious autumnal day, however, as I nervously joined the other new students chatting outside the Dean's office, neither of those skills seemed to be particularly useful attributes for a career in medicine.

Named after a famous alumnus, the Nevin lecture theatre was directly opposite the Dean's office. It lay to the left of a wide corridor, which connected the main entrance to the hospital – on Lambeth Palace Road – to the old Victorian ward block on the banks of the Thames. Alongside the double doors, which constituted the main entrance to the lecture theatre, there was a notice board announcing the week's lectures and in front of this a small waiting area with a few chairs; and it was here that we had been instructed to congregate. Around me, standing or seated, were about thirty other young men and a few women, all talking loudly and confidently on seemingly erudite topics. They all appeared to be entirely at ease, indeed excited, in this new arcane environment; but I was not. The girls in particular made me feel self-conscious and uneasy.

In one corner of this waiting area I spotted Arthur, my new room-mate, chatting animatedly to a tall young man. Arthur's shirt was unbuttoned at the neck but on this beautifully sunny afternoon he was still wearing the short beige raincoat that he had arrived in the day before. Grasped firmly in his right hand was a briefcase.

'Y'know,' Arthur said, smiling confidently at his new acquaintance, 'I think the great thing about leaving school and being a student is not having to wear a blasted collar and tie all the time.' The tall individual he was addressing – who hadn't made the complete transition from school tie to open neck and was wearing a cravat – just nodded slowly in agreement. Arthur continued, 'Of course, we used to have to wear those separate starched collars attached by studs. You know, the ones that go soggy in the rain.'

'Really?' was all the tall young man said as he continued to nod, somewhat puzzled by the topic of conversation and Arthur's attire.

Sensing this, Arthur continued authoritatively, 'That's why I always choose to wear a raincoat and carry an umbrella,' adding, 'London is particularly unpredictable – weather-wise.' Then, to demonstrate his preparedness for a sudden change in climatic conditions, he proceeded to open his briefcase and from it withdrew a telescopic umbrella. Not content merely to prove that he always carried this about his person, Arthur then pressed a button on its shaft, whereupon it suddenly doubled in length and the canopy of the umbrella began slowly to unfurl. The confined space in which we were standing was not the best place to demonstrate the undoubtedly useful attributes of the self-opening umbrella and it became entangled in the hair of a pretty girl standing behind him. Apologising profusely to the startled young woman, Arthur disentangled the brolly from her head while attempting to pat her hair back in place. With the young lady placated, he folded it up expertly and replaced it in his briefcase. Until then I had been standing conspicuously alone, too embarrassed to talk to anyone but now, reassured in some perverse way by the umbrella incident, I took the opportunity to join this duo whose conversation didn't appear to be too challenging.

'Hi, I'm Grahame,' I said nervously, extending my hand to the tall young man, then for some reason adding, 'I'm from

Norwich,' as though that would immediately make me a more interesting person.

'Hello, my name is William.' This was articulated in an unmistakable public school accent, very slowly and precisely. At six foot four it was unusual for *me* to have to look up at anyone, but he was taller than me by about an inch. He had short fair hair with just a hint of ginger and in addition to wearing a cravat tucked into his Viyella checked shirt he wore a sports jacket, cavalry twill trousers and highly polished brown boots.

'I'm from Burton where the best beer in England is brewed,' he added slowly with a smile. Here at last, I thought, was someone to whom I could relate, and I was about to expound on the excellence of certain Norfolk ales when a tweedy middle-aged lady came out from the Dean's office and announced that we should now register.

* * *

It had been only ten months earlier that I had been standing outside the selfsame lecture theatre waiting to be interviewed for a place at this famous London medical school. On that December day, London had been very different: draughty and cold, its pavements reflecting the sky with the dampness of a recent shower. I had been wearing an ill-fitting suit – well, not actually a suit at all but simply a charcoal-grey jacket and trousers of a similar shade. The poor fit and the difference in the colours were sufficient to make the statement, 'I am not from a privileged background, but I *have* made an effort'. My mother, the 'Zomp', had said that I looked very smart as I left that morning to catch the train from Norwich to Liverpool Street. My interview was scheduled for the early afternoon and I'd arrived in ample time.

I timidly knocked at a door marked 'Dean's Office' which was subsequently opened by a pleasant lady in her forties wearing a tweed jacket and skirt. 'Good afternoon. I'm Grahame Howard,' I said, introducing myself. 'I'm here for an interview.'

'Ah yes, Mr Howard, we're running a bit late. Do please take a seat,' she replied, gesturing towards a row of spindly chairs ranged against the wall. Opposite, there was another door on which a notice proclaimed, *Silence Please. Interview in Progress*. As the lady settled back to her typewriter, I sat down and stared miserably out of the rain-bespattered window towards the Houses of Parliament on the opposite bank of the Thames. I wanted to be anywhere but where I was. I had been to and from the toilet about five times since arriving at the hospital an hour before, the last time being ten minutes ago, but this unexpected delay made me wonder if I should go again and, if so, whether there would be time. While I was pondering the options I heard the muffled tinkle of a bell from inside the interview room.

'You may go in now,' said the lady with a smile as she rose from her desk and opened the door to usher me in. As I passed, I heard her whisper, 'Good luck! Don't be nervous.' I entered the room, which was warm and filled with slightly stale air. The single window – through which the opposite bank of the Thames was just discernible through the dark and threatening sky – was closed. Facing me was a heavy, well-polished mahogany table, behind which sat the panel of four men. I took a few steps into the room and stood awkwardly with my arms stiffly by my side.

'Good afternoon,' I said, with rather more confidence than I was feeling.

'Mr Howard?'

'Yes, sir,' I replied. The speaker was a bespectacled, grey-haired man in a three-piece pin-striped suit, on the shoulders of which were small specks of dandruff. As he looked up at me, he removed his glasses and with just a hint of a smile used them to gesture toward a vacant chair opposite him. This I took as an invitation to sit down.

With his glasses once more perched on the end of his nose, he peered at the papers on the table in front of him and then, looking directly at me, asked in a business-like fashion, 'Now, Mr. Howard, why is it that you want to be a doctor?' I had already rehearsed a variety of answers to this predictable question, trying to achieve the right balance of sincerity without sounding pretentious. It was easy to offer a pat response – much harder to seem honest and credible.

'I'm not entirely sure if there is any *one* particular reason,' I explained, 'but I do know that it is the only career I have wanted to follow since I was about twelve years old.'

'Any idea of what being a doctor entails?'

'My uncle was a doctor; my cousin is a medical student and I have discussed this ambition with my G.P. at home in Norwich. I'm confident that medicine is what I want to do.' I didn't think it was necessary to say that the 'uncle' I referred to had qualified in 1921 and had died just two years later.

The members of the panel were all very polite and friendly, taking it in turn to ask a number of questions, some of which I was fully prepared for. I began to breathe more easily and my urge to go to the toilet had disappeared.

'Why did you apply to St Thomas' as your first choice?' This was such an obvious question that I had rehearsed several answers, none of which was particularly convincing. The honest answer was that when I submitted my application, I made St Thomas' my preferred option as it was the only London medical school I hadn't previously heard of. This was the rather dubious logic for thinking that it might be the institution most likely to accept me. Everyone had heard of Guy's and Bart's and I had judged there was little hope of gaining admission to either of those famous institutions. Clearly, however, such honesty would scarcely have been appropriate. When discussing this with the Zomp, she had said we once had an aunt who had trained at the famous Nightingale School of nursing, and so I now explained that this somewhat tenuous family connection was my main reason for choosing St Thomas'. That seemed to be an adequate response and the questioner then passed me on to one of his colleagues, a large handsome man – an orthopaedic surgeon whom I later learned had played rugby for Scotland.

'Do you think you'll be playing for the first fifteen by the end of the season?' he asked innocently – or so it seemed to me. Suddenly the atmosphere in the room changed. All the interviewers seemed to be holding their breath. The paper-shuffling ceased abruptly and all eyes were focused on me. It seemed that the light in the room had dimmed, the temperature had dropped a degree or two and my urge to go to the toilet had returned. I sensed there was only one correct answer to this question. In reality there was no chance of my playing for the firsts that season – or indeed any other. I had stretched the truth considerably in my application by stating that I was playing for the Second Fifteen, when in truth I had only come on once as a substitute.

'Yes, I would certainly hope so, sir.' I replied emphatically.

There was an almost audible sigh of relief from the interviewers who went back to shuffling their papers and gazing out over the Thames. It had been the right answer and the tension in the room eased. The rest of the interview seemed a formality.

'Why don't you want to go to music school?'

I was prepared for that one. 'The only reason I'd want to study music is if I could become a concert pianist and I'm just not good enough. It will always be a hobby of mine though,' I added.

All seemed to be going well; then came a problem.

'You do realise, don't you, that you're really too young to start with the next intake? You'll only just be seventeen by then?'

The questioner peered at me over his half-moon spectacles. In fact I'd had no idea I was too young. I'd simply assumed that entry was secure provided one had passed sufficient A-levels and had been accepted by the panel.

'It's a long course,' I replied, 'and I'd be very keen to start as soon as possible – that is, if I'm lucky enough to be accepted.'

That proved to be sufficient and back at home in Norwich a few days later I was overjoyed to receive a letter offering me a place for the following academic session. All I needed was to secure 3 A-levels and achieve an average C grade.

* * *

The problem was that my final year at school in the upper sixth was fun – too much fun. The whole year was dedicated, heart and soul, to trying to lose my virginity. Although the pack of three condoms I had bought two years earlier remained unused, I felt sure it couldn't be long before they would be needed. Meeting girls and trying to get off with one was the number one – no, the *only* – priority. There were parties nearly every weekend and whether invited or not you wouldn't be refused entry, provided you pitched up with a drink, usually a Watney's Party Four. Bruce had used the same Party Four for about six months. After gaining entry to the party, he would then hide the large can in a suitable cupboard and at the end of the evening retrieve it for use on a subsequent occasion. This worked well until he appeared at one party rather late when all the alcoholic beverages had already been consumed. Gratefully, the can was taken from him immediately on arrival and he could only watch, stunned and unbelieving, as all the contents were rapidly devoured before his very eyes. He was so unsettled by the experience that it was some time before he attempted that manoeuvre again.

My own life was, of course, wholly preoccupied with the idea of sex. This was uncharted territory for me and I was so naïve that I firmly believed that the only way to have sex with a girl was to catch one off-guard. The other problem was that I was so shy that I needed at least six or seven pints of beer before I could summon up the courage even to speak to a member of the opposite sex. This was also the time of Watney's Starlight, a beer so weak and diuretic that it was virtually impossible to benefit from the disinhibiting effect of the alcohol without having to spend most of the evening in the Gents. This exquisite shyness, coupled with my inability even to speak to a girl without consuming a gallon of beer first, were distinct disabilities that were to dominate my social life for some years.

In my futile search for sex, I explored every opportunity I could find that might result in any kind of contact with girls. I joined sixth-form societies, went to folk clubs and, as well as gate-crashing parties, even resorted to attending school dances. These were invariably dire and poorly supported – by girls at any rate. Smithie and I decided that it would improve attendance (while at the same time massively improving our standing in the eyes of the High School girls) if we invited somebody famous to one of our sixth-form dances. Accordingly, we sent an invitation – along with a free ticket and travel directions – to Princess Anne. We received a polite but firm reply stating that Her Royal Highness had a prior engagement and would not be able to attend. After this initial disappointment we sent an invitation to Diana Rigg. Amazingly she apparently had a prior engagement as well – what atrocious luck, we thought. At least we received a picture of Miss Rigg, in a slightly provocative pose, which we rented out for a shilling a day.

It was probably the potentially explosive combination of testosterone and alcohol that resulted in us sometimes perpetrating reckless and puerile pranks. Smithie was a practised practical joker. He started young when, as an impish seven year-old, he had placed a realistic plastic turd in my desk during lunch-break. When I opened my desk to retrieve my books for the first lesson of the afternoon I saw it and froze. The turd was sitting neatly coiled on the exercise book that I required, and I found myself unable either to reach inside, or to close the desk. Mrs Frith, our teacher, asked me what was wrong. I was speechless and motionless, rooted to the spot; half-standing, half-sitting, my desk-lid held open, my eyes wide, fixated on its interior. I couldn't understand how a turd (I thought it was real) could have found its way into my desk over lunch. Failing to get a response from me, Mrs Frith bustled over, and on seeing the contents of my desk, stormed out of the classroom without a word. She returned shortly with some toilet paper, and using this, removed the offending item and placed it in the bin. Smithie received six of the best for this prank, but he was undeterred and just became more skilled at avoiding detection.

Thus it was a more mature and sophisticated Smithie who some ten years later, decided to phone the Drug Squad, tipping them off that there were drugs at a party and giving the address of the senior masters' common-room in the Cathedral Close. On their arrival the police burst in, interrupting the headmaster and his colleagues, formally gowned and enjoying their pre-prandial sherry. I am not entirely sure who was the more surprised – masters or policemen. Next morning questions were asked at Assembly, but the culprit was never found.

The 'Adam and Eve' is a delightful flint building and lays claim to being the oldest public house in Norwich. It is situated just outside the Cathedral Close, a short walk from Norwich School and it was thus to this pub that we habitually retired after our failed seduction attempts. After one of our many spectacularly unsuccessful evenings, as closing time approached, four of us were disconsolately finishing our pints when Bruce suddenly sat bolt upright, a gleam in his eye, 'I know, chaps, why don't we go and swap some gates?' he said. To a man, we all turned our eyes upon the speaker, convinced that Bruce had finally lost his already tenuous link with reality. Gradually, however, the attractiveness of his plan began to dawn upon each of us. Bruce had concocted some less than good ideas in the past and indeed was to have some in the future – including the occasion some years later when, as a trainee accountant, he caused mayhem trying to find out how much a prostitute would charge for sex.

In suburban Norwich many houses had wrought-iron gates, which could readily be lifted off their hinges and swapped with a similar gate further along the road, and on previous occasions this had proved to be good sport.

'Nice one, Bruce,' I said, and so we finished our pints and headed for the prime gate-swapping region of North Norwich. It was about midnight when, after we had swapped a few gates, two homeowners – on hearing the scrapes and squeaks as each gate was lifted and replaced by another – came out to investigate. Initially they were puzzled as they looked at their gates and tried to discover what exactly was different. One of them began to accuse the other of taking his gate and we slipped away unnoticed as an unseemly altercation ensued. What wasn't so clever was that we then moved to Constitution Hill, where I lived, and repeated the process. My friend Paul must have lost his presence of mind completely when he actually swapped his own gates with those of a neighbour.

All of this partying and drinking was not conducive to optimal preparation for the impending A-level examinations and I was lucky to achieve the grades required by a narrow margin. After some final weeks in Norwich, the last ever when No. 3 Constitution Hill could truly be called my home, Dod drove me down to London one quiet Sunday afternoon. I had missed the opportunity to secure a place in a hall of residence so was allocated a room in shared digs within a red brick late Edwardian semi-detached house in Topsham Road, Tooting. The family were very welcoming but, once Dod and I had parted, the enormity of what was happening suddenly hit me – the Spoz had left home for good.

As I sat quietly on one of the two single beds in my new bedroom, wondering what to do next, I heard the doorbell ring. The door was opened and I overheard the landlord welcoming someone. I descended the steep flight of stairs and caught my first glimpse of Arthur, my room-mate to be, and a future stalwart friend. He was of medium height and slim built, with short, straight, straw-coloured hair, which flopped over his right eye. He had a soft, beardless, slightly podgy face, with full lips which seemed somewhat too large. He was wearing a light-coloured raincoat under which he sported an open-necked shirt and jeans, while on his feet were suede desert boots. As I reached the small hallway at the foot of the stairs, I extended my hand. 'Hi, I'm

Grahame Howard,' I said. His handshake was slightly limp, but his response was in a deep, rich, resonant voice. 'Hello, I'm Arthur Wilkinson.' He turned towards a slim, middle-aged man wearing a white shirt, crested tie and sports jacket, and added, 'This is my father.' I shook his hand.

'Are you starting at St Thomas' as well?' he asked with a refined but clearly discernible Yorkshire accent.

'Yes I am.'

'Well done!' he said, continuing to shake my hand vigorously and then, turning to his son, added, 'I said to Arthur 'ere, that he's done well to be accepted, but that's just the start. There's long hard graft ahead of 'im.' This cheered me up no end and I stood aside to allow Arthur and his father to carry a large wooden box and two suitcases upstairs to the bedroom. Father and son then exchanged a stiff handshake. 'Well, son, I know they'll work you 'ard at St Thomas'. Stick at it.' He then turned on his heel and was gone. Arthur had been a boarder at a famous public school and immediately set about arranging his half of our shared room to his liking, just as though he was back in his dormitory. Having been a day-boy myself, I was unused to sharing personal space. Horrified at the idea, I did the only thing I could think of: I went in search of the nearest pub.

The following day, after a troubled night's sleep, disturbed by Arthur's snoring and my own numerous trips to the bathroom, I travelled with him to St Thomas' to register and found myself outside the Nevin lecture theatre, feeling quite alone and isolated.

CHAPTER 2:

SKELETONS AND CADAVERS

At half past ten precisely, the slightly prim middle-aged, grey-haired lady – the one who had whispered, 'Good luck' to me before my interview the year before – appeared in the waiting area. Now she appeared rather less sympathetic, for we were to be her charges for the next five years. After scrutinising us rather disapprovingly for a few seconds, she then clapped her hands, rather as a primary school teacher would do, when summoning the children in from their play. The hubbub of conversation gradually diminished and after a second clap of her hands she announced, 'Ladies and gentlemen, would you come and register. In an *orderly* fashion, please?' So saying, she directed us into the Dean's suite of offices where we formed an untidy line, while the excited hubbub started up once more. Eventually I reached the head of the queue and so took my turn to register.

'May I have your name, please?' The tweedy lady looked up, and smiled at me with a hint of recognition, and a rather maternal look on her face.

'Howard; Grahame Howard.'

'And is your date of birth the fifteenth of May, 1953?'

'Yes.'

'You're very young: only just seventeen. Do you have somewhere to live?'

'Yes, thank you. I'm in digs at Tooting.' I gave her the address.

'Here are the details of the course, including your first term's lectures, and you will need to buy a few things such as a laboratory coat before you start tomorrow. The list of essentials is in here.' She looked up as she handed me a bulky folder. 'Don't look so worried. You'll be fine!' she smiled. 'St Thomas' House is just to the left, down the ramp as you go out by the door in the corridor. Now do get yourself a coffee – you look as though you need one.' So saying, she turned her attention to the next student in the queue. 'And *your* name, please?'

Folder in hand, I stepped out of the Hospital into the sunshine and walked the fifty yards to St Thomas' House. Hesitantly, I mounted the four broad stone steps in front of the imposing main entrance to this Victorian building which would become the hub of my social life for the next six years. I pushed open one of the two heavy glass-panelled doors and entered, exchanging the warmth of the late summer sun for the cool dimness of the main vestibule. Looming over me from the walls hung dark, claustrophobic wooden panels, listing, in faded gilt lettering, the names of innumerable sportsmen from previous years. Directly ahead was the Porters' Lodge. This, I discovered, was Ron's territory. It was a small office with a sliding glass window, behind which I could see a man in a white linen jacket reading a tabloid newspaper. He was of indeterminate age – neither young nor old. He had slicked-down greying hair and on his large, rather rubbery face there was perched a pair of tortoiseshell glasses set at a somewhat peculiar angle. I didn't like to disturb him, but he was clearly some kind of gatekeeper and I thought it only polite to ask his permission to enter. I knocked gently on the glass partition. After a considerable delay, Ron slowly removed his reading glasses and looked up to identify the cause of this intrusion. On seeing me, he very deliberately set down his paper, and with a tired expression stood up and slid open the glass partition.

'Yes, *squire*?' he said slowly, with heavy emphasis on the title 'squire'.

'Awfully sorry to trouble you, but I'm a new student and I'm looking for the canteen.'

'That way, *squire*,' he said, nodding towards another set of double doors to his left. So saying, he firmly closed the glass hatch, resumed his seat, picked up the newspaper and, after re-adjusting his spectacles, carried on reading. I later discovered that Ron popped up in various places at different times of the day. At one p.m. he would station himself in the white coat store, dishing out short white coats to the clinical students, and from four o'clock onwards he took on the role of barman until closing time at eight each evening. Rumour had it that in a previous life he had been a professional boxer and on occasions had used his pugilistic skills to expel unwanted guests and drunken students.

To my right was a broad and winding staircase ascending to the first floor, the stairwell lined with a continuation of the wooden plaques, laden with still more gilded names. On that floor was sited the main lounge – a long, pillared room with a high ceiling and polished wooden floors, partially covered by two huge Persian carpets on which were placed four or five comfortable settees. The all-important bar was to the left of the entrance and at the far end of the room was a stage. The upper two floors housed accommodation for final year students and those doing student clerkships.

With a final glance at Ron I hesitantly entered the canteen. At length, finding a vacant table in a dark corner where I hoped to remain quite unobserved, I sat down and opened my folder. It contained details of the course, a daunting reading list of some ten books, including *Gray's Anatomy*, along with advice on how to obtain other items such as a skeleton, a dissection kit and a white laboratory coat. One problem was immediately apparent – something which was to dog me for the rest of my student career and indeed for most of my life: I didn't have enough money. I could never afford to buy all the recommended books and the other necessary items, while also paying a term in advance for my digs and leaving some money for essentials like food – let alone luxuries such as beer and cigarettes. I decided to share my concerns with the other new boys – assuming that they would surely have similar financial worries. I summoned up the courage to buy myself a coffee and joined a group of fellow-students who were chatting loudly at an adjacent table.

'Hi. Mind if I join you?'

'Hello, again. Yes, please do.' I recognised the slow, deliberate voice immediately. It was William whom I had met earlier. He introduced me to the others around the table, all of whom he seemed to know quite well. He then continued the point he'd been making prior to my interruption. 'You see, the difference between a doctor and all other professions is that *he* or she, is the only one who has a licence to view someone naked.' I was hugely impressed by this thoughtful analysis and began to wonder if this applied to medical students – with particular regard to nurses. The discussion rambled on, and then there came a lull in the conversation. I grasped the opportunity: 'Do you think we need to buy *all* these books?' I asked no one in particular, brandishing the book list. 'They'll cost a *fortune*!'

'*I've* bought them all.' Arthur brushed the straw hair from his eyes, only for it to fall back immediately. 'I asked for the reading list to be sent to me at home in Leeds, and bought them all there. All *I* need now is a skeleton.'

'Luckily, my father still had *his* books,' volunteered one dark-haired, good-looking young man from the other end of the table. Like William, he sported a cravat and had been puffing gently on a pipe. 'Maybe a bit out of date, but anatomy hasn't changed that much, I imagine.' He said this in a very lazy but refined accent, his face creasing as he smiled gently and replaced the pipe in his mouth. A ripple of laughter travelled around the table, it was evident that no one else seemed to have the slightest financial concerns.

We talked for a while, then having finished his coffee, the man who had inherited his father's books put his still-smoking pipe in the right-hand hip pocket of his sports jacket and announced, 'Well, I'm off to buy a white coat and a dissection kit. Anyone want to join me?'

He seemed to know where he was going, so about six of us set off together, with me tagging along at the back of the group. We walked the short distance along Lambeth Palace Road to Westminster Bridge and then along York Road, eventually reaching a rather dingy-looking shop beneath some railway arches near Waterloo Station. Here we each purchased a laboratory coat and dissection kit. With my essential shopping done, I took my leave and headed to the Underground and caught a tube train to Tooting Bec from where I trudged the half-mile to my digs. I hadn't seen Arthur since we had left St Thomas' House when he had set off in the opposite direction from the rest of us. As I opened the front door, there he stood, half-way up the stairs, struggling to drag a heavy wooden box up to our room. At the sound of the front door opening, he turned.

'Ah, Grahame. Perfect timing. Give me a hand with this, would you?' I grabbed the rope handle at one end of the box and we carried it up the remaining steps to our bedroom where we dumped it on the floor.

'Gosh!' Arthur was panting after the exertions of manhandling the box all the way from the shop on Charing Cross Road where he had purchased his skeleton. 'These skeletons are damned heavy things. Now, let's see what we've got. Important not to fall behind with Anatomy, don't you think?' He opened the box and settled down to identify some bones with the help of the illustrations in one of the textbooks he had brought with him from Yorkshire. 'Absolutely,' I replied, with my confidence rapidly waning. I had already calculated that I couldn't possibly afford a skeleton and hadn't even yet bought any books; so all I could do was try on my laboratory coat and admire my dissection kit.

Already I felt doomed to failure. Arthur seemed to know everything, and his natural composure and exuberance brought out the opposite characteristics in me. He was a typically self-confident specimen of the public school system, having learned to fend for himself from an early age – during term time at least. Though irritatingly confident, he had many excellent qualities, including an innate sense of fairness, an ability to work in a team, and leadership skills. Rather less endearing was his habit of picking his nose and eating the contents, which was probably why he later became known as 'von Mucus-Eater'. It was some time before I discovered that Arthur was not so infallible as I'd first thought – but his sense of responsibility and fairness, along with his basic concern for others, prevailed for as long as I knew him.

Next day, after an early breakfast, we set off together for our first full day as students. As we walked along Topsham Road toward Tooting Bec Station, Arthur was once again extolling the virtues of his collapsible umbrella, when ahead of us a shabbily-dressed elderly man spat profusely on the pavement. 'Most common way of transmitting tuberculosis, that,' exclaimed Arthur authoritatively as we passed the spot, while at the same time demonstrating how the collapsible umbrella could neatly be inserted into his briefcase in one easy, fluent movement. I was most impressed, possessing neither a briefcase nor an umbrella – collapsible or otherwise.

The St Thomas' pre-clinical course was underpinned by a detailed study of the gross anatomy of the human body. A previous member of staff had edited *Gray's Anatomy* and some two-thirds of our time was dedicated to this subject. It was thus no surprise that our first morning as medical students was to be spent in the dissection room. I suspect that none of us had ever seen a dead body before and it was with considerable apprehension that we shuffled into the cold, museum-like room where the cadavers lay awaiting our attention. As I passed through the heavy wooden doors, the first thing that struck me was the smell – the overpowering, all-pervading smell of formaldehyde, followed by the inevitable irritation to my eyes and throat. I coughed and had to halt momentarily just inside the room to wipe the tears from my eyes. Once recovered, I replaced my spectacles and looked around. There were three rows of four metal tables, each covered by a sheet with its undulations conforming to the ghostly outline of a human form. At the end of the room nearest to us was a long porcelain sink with half a dozen taps, and soap dispensers attached to the wall behind. I followed the others to a notice board where, typed on a piece of paper, were the names of the students allocated to each cadaver. Having identified my group I slowly made my way across the room to the table in the far right-hand corner to meet my new colleagues who were already congregated there.

Each group of five students was allocated one cadaver to be dissected over the subsequent eighteen months. My team comprised four men, all sharing a surname beginning with H, together with one short, frizzy-haired, tomboyish girl called Joan who looked about twelve, and must have been even more apprehensive than the rest of us. We introduced ourselves. Mike resembled a pop star. Good-looking, with shoulder-length wavy blond hair, he was the shortest of us men, at about five foot six, but was stylishly dressed in designer jeans and a tight-fitting open-necked shirt under his laboratory coat. Having said 'Hello', to him, I turned to shake hands with the man alongside. He also was expensively dressed, but in a more traditional style. He had dark short hair, a neatly-trimmed beard and looked slightly older than the rest of us, being probably in his early twenties.

'Eddie,' he said, shaking my hand. Then, in a perfect imitation of Derek Guyler's northern accent, he added, 'I was in the Desert Rats y'know.'

I was a bit taken aback. 'I beg your pardon?'

'I was in the Desert Rats y'know,' he said again, this time pretending to play a clarinet.

The third 'H' at the table, Pete, said, 'Don't worry about him. He's been saying that all morning. He thinks he's a cross between Derek Guyler and Artie Shaw.'

'Oh!' I said. 'Hi. I'm Grahame Howard.'

After these brief introductions we fell silent and all of us looked nervously at the white sheet with its human-like form on

35

the metal table in front of us. Long gone were the days of Burke and Hare and the resurrectionists; beneath the sheet was a man who had bequeathed his mortal remains to the medical school while he was still alive.

'Well, I think we need to take a look.' It was the girl, Joan, who stepped forward and gradually removed the sheet, first revealing the head and then the torso of the cadaver. She stood back and we all gazed in silence at the body of an emaciated old man lying on the cold steel table. Around his head was a thin halo of grey hair; his nose was squashed to one side and he had that peculiar grey tinge that only preserved bodies have. I began to wonder about this man. Criminal, lawyer, tramp? Anatomically they were all the same. Blood vessels ran in the same direction and the organs worked – or not, as the case might be. I asked myself what made us different when we were alive? Fat or thin, rich or poor, stupid or wise – we were all levelled when laid out on the slab.

'Well, then. Who's going to start?' Pete interrupted my musings.

In our pristine white coats and with our new dissection kits unrolled on the shelf behind us we all hesitated, pretending to study our manuals. Dissection was to begin on the arm but none of us wanted to make the first cut.

'You do it, Joan,' I said, as she had clearly shown the greatest initiative thus far.

'No. I took the sheet off.' She was not to be persuaded. Eddie pretended to play the opening bars from Gershwin's Rhapsody in Blue in the style of Artie Shaw, a strange noise emanating from his pursed lips.

As the rest of us hesitated, Mike said, 'Right, I'll do it,' and, scalpel in hand, he stepped forward and made a timid incision over the shoulder, so exposing the brown fibres of the muscle underneath. We had taken the first step.

As we observed this first cut and examined our manuals to discover what to do next, a slim, short, dapper man with neat

Brylcreemed jet-black hair and a toothbrush moustache strolled slowly across the room towards us. He was wearing a well-cut dark suit, while dangling from his mouth was a lighted Senior Service non-tipped cigarette. He stopped at our table and peered at Mike's incision. 'I'm Dr Trimble, your tutor,' he announced, almost in a whisper. 'What's that?' He had taken the cigarette out of his mouth and was using it to point toward the muscle that had just been exposed.

Tremulously, Mike responded, 'I think it's the deltoid muscle, sir.'

'Very good. Do carry on.' Dr Trimble said this quietly with the faintest of smiles; then without a further word he strolled slowly to the next table, leaving a pall of cigarette smoke in his wake.

Dr Trimble was an extraordinary man. Married to a ballet dancer, he chain-smoked Senior Service cigarettes and told us that his greatest claim to fame was that he had once gone fishing with a Nobel Laureate. A gifted artist, his tutorials might well have been an art class. He would begin by sketching a bone in white chalk on the blackboard and then adding other structures as he talked and smoked – brown muscles, red arteries, blue veins – until the whole structure sprang into being. I truly hated to see him carelessly rub out these masterpieces at the end of each session. He taught us about sartorius, the muscle that helps us cross our legs, and how it was named after the tailors who used to sit cross-legged; and about gracilis, the muscle that brings our legs together, very aptly named the virgin's muscle; and how the psoas muscle in the cow provides us with that most tender and expensive cut of meat, the fillet steak. He also explained how falling asleep in a chair with arms outstretched (usually when inebriated) could lead to radial nerve paralysis – the so-called Friday night palsy.

Dissection was enjoyable. Joan and the other three 'H's proved excellent company and we soon became close friends. Eddie's slightly eccentric behaviour masked his inherent shyness.

In addition to being able to imitate Derek Guyler to perfection, he was a talented clarinetist, a fervent admirer of Artie Shaw, and we would later play duets together. Pete introduced us to a whole new style of dark, irreverent humour particularly suited to the dissection room.

There were three other subjects which were to dominate our lives for the next eighteen months. Histology involved spending long hours peering into microscopes at unrecognisable red and green dots. This was soporific in the extreme and as a result could be quite dangerous. The eyepiece of a microscope is just about the same diameter as one's eye socket – for obvious reasons – but this meant that if, as you nodded off, your head dropped forward, the eyepiece of the microscope could penetrate quite a distance into your skull before the ensuing discomfort wakened you. Permanent injury was generally avoided, but black eyes did occur – and of course this became even more of a problem when binocular microscopes were introduced.

The other pre-clinical subjects with which we filled our week were biochemistry and physiology. Biochemistry seemed to be about of lots of cycles. Not of the two-wheel variety, but diagrams consisting of a myriad of lines – straight and curved – with arrows radiating towards indecipherable symbols and acronyms. Within this chaos there were numerous plus and minus signs, with letters whizzing off in all directions. Those diagrams looked rather like a plate of spaghetti, or lots of merry-go-rounds, all tangled, with the passengers shooting from one ride to another.

Physiology was altogether more fun. Here we had to push tubes into each other's orifices and extract the juices, as well as take blood and other body fluids for analysis. Many of these experiments required volunteers to have various indignities inflicted on them. I had to swallow a naso-gastric tube and have my stomach contents aspirated, while William had a proctoscope inserted into his anus while the rest of the class took turns to look inside. In order to demonstrate that the blush response affected the lower bowel as well as the face, he was told that a particularly pretty girl was having a peek, and (as predicted) the inside of his rectum turned as red as his face. There was only one experiment for which all of us volunteered, and that was to measure the effect of alcohol on our response times. Unfortunately, those of us who were known to drink and had therefore induced their liver enzymes to reach a high state of readiness were excluded – since only inexperienced drinkers were suitable subjects for this experiment. Two or three cans of beer later, those poor unfortunates – normally timid and bashful – were swaggering around the lab belching, swearing and making lewd comments to the female students. One of them even had to be helped home – all in the name of science.

For coffee breaks and lunch, we would walk the fifty yards or so from the pre-clinical school to the canteen at St Thomas' House. My fees and digs were paid for, but this left very little for other essentials such as beer or cigarettes. As a result of this chronic shortage of money, I ate as frugally as possible, knowing that I would have at least one solid meal each day back at my digs.

I quickly became accustomed to the routine of lectures, experiments and the daily commute from Tooting to Waterloo. Occasionally, I would have a beer with Arthur or William but socially things were far from exciting. My condoms remained unused and the girls in my year were all so intelligent and confident that in their presence I became little more than a gibbering idiot.

From our very first day as medical students we had discovered the pleasures and camaraderie of the bar in St Thomas' House. It was there one evening, while we were having a quiet beer after the day's lectures, that Arthur and I began moaning to William about the disadvantages of living in Tooting.

'Why don't you chaps apply to one of the halls of residence? It would save a lot of travelling and it would be much more fun than living so far away.' In saying this William had a point.

Arthur and I both agreed that our digs were not ideal. Although we got on very well together in general, sharing the same small space for leisure, study and sleep was becoming claustrophobic for both of us.

'It would be nice to become more independent and have one's own room,' Arthur said, stroking the fair hair out of his eyes. 'And once in Tooting there's nothing at all to do. Even the local pub's pretty boring.'

'Why don't you apply to the hall that I'm in; or there's another one, Liverpool Hall, just along the road. It would be great fun if we lived close together, *and* you'd have your own room. You might even get lucky, if you know what I mean?' William leered at me.

Neither Arthur nor I had a girlfriend yet and it was clear to us that living nearly an hour's tube trip from the centre of London and sharing a bedroom reduced the odds of successful seduction to just about zero. There were also other irritations. Our landlords were a young married couple who obviously needed the money. The wife was Italian and, in fairness, she did teach us how to eat spaghetti without dropping most of it on to our shirts or into our laps, a skill which I seem to have lost as I've grown older. True, we were guaranteed a meal each evening, which was served at six o'clock precisely, following which we were allowed to watch the family television for a short time, but thereafter we were expected to retire to our shared room for study.

As the term progressed, this rigid timetable grew to be increasingly frustrating. Sharing a room was becoming unacceptable to both Arthur and myself and it became apparent that a move was necessary. Accordingly, we took William's advice and at the end of our first term were fortunate enough to secure places in Liverpool Hall – a hall of residence near King's Cross. Now perhaps I could blossom and, with my new-found independence and a room to myself, those condoms would surely be required soon.

CHAPTER 3:

LAW AND DISORDER

On moving into Liverpool Hall I felt that I had, at last, truly broken away from the constraints of parental care and become a student in the proper sense of the word. I had my own study bedroom, there was a large dining room – where we congregated for breakfast and dinner – a junior common room, a bar, and a television room where we could watch programmes as late into the night as we wished. *Star Trek* and *Top of the Pops* were essential viewing and *Without You* by Harry Nielsen was at number one in the charts. At the nearby Kings Cross Cinema the double bill was *The Graduate* and *Butch Cassidy and the Sundance Kid*. I befriended an eclectic mix of students from different backgrounds and religious persuasions, many nationalities and colours, reading for all manner of degrees. The only variety of student I couldn't befriend was one of the opposite sex, since a prerequisite for entry to Liverpool Hall was that one was male. Hence, this was an all-male residence – or so I thought – until the fire alarm went off once in the middle of the night and we had to evacuate the building. I was surprised to find how many sisters and mothers of the residents – as these were the only female guests allowed – had stayed late into the night.

William and some other students from St Thomas' lived in a another hall of residence just a hundred yards away at the other end of Cartwright Gardens while, sandwiched in between these two all-male bastions, was Russell Hall for young ladies. To say that it had barbed wire surrounding it would be to overstate the case somewhat, but access for males was strictly limited to attendance for specific events, such as their film club – when we would be counted in and counted out. Apart from those occasions, Russell Hall was an impenetrable fortress. Of course we made attempts to enter illegally, but were always discovered and escorted off the premises by the warden. Being forcibly ejected from an all-female establishment was an occurrence that would prove to be repeated some years later – but on that occasion it was to be from a nurses' home, and our escorts were to be the police.

Living in nearby halls of residence meant that Arthur and I saw a lot of William and his friends and most weekends we would meet to explore the local pubs, invariably finishing up with fish and chips from the nearby North Sea Fish Bar. After a night's drinking it was traditional to carry home some souvenirs of the evening. Traffic signs, yellow flashing lights and the like were all considered desirable accessories to help furnish our rather sparse rooms.

On one such night, as we wandered home after an evening imbibing a few ales in a number of pleasant hostelries around nearby Queen's Square, William spotted a foreign number plate on the rear of a parked car.

'Gosh! Look at that. I think it's German. That would look great on my wall, just above the ONE WAY ONLY sign.' In his excitement William was speaking slightly faster than was usual for him, and, with the briefest of glances over his shoulder, walked over to the car and attempted to wrench off the number plate. Arthur and I waited on the pavement a few yards away, pretending not to be party to this misdemeanour.

'You're making far too much noise. Shush! Be quieter, William,' hissed Arthur, who was becoming increasingly anxious and began looking nervously up and down the otherwise quiet side-street.

'Give me a hand then, you two,' William whispered loudly. Arthur and I joined him and after some crude tugging and twisting the number plate finally came away from the car. William looked at it with considerable pride as he brushed it clean with the sleeve of his sports jacket. He then realised that his souvenir was much larger than at first appeared and was proving to be extremely difficult to conceal. After a struggle he succeeded in hiding most of it under his jacket, which he buttoned up tightly to hold it in place.

'Good! For heaven's sake, let's get back now,' I said, beginning to walk briskly in the direction of Cartwright Gardens.

I'm not certain which of us first noticed the short, overweight, middle-aged man walking in our direction, but we chose to ignore him until he was within a few yards of us, which was to prove an error. Suddenly he called out, 'Oi! You three. What are you lads up to?'

'Just going home,' we mumbled in unison, unconcerned.

'I'm an off-duty police officer.'

On hearing this, my heart sank and I heard Arthur mutter, 'Shit!'

The policeman was now only a few feet away from us. 'What's that you've got inside your jacket?' he demanded, pointing at William, who promptly feigned complete surprise at discovering that somehow a car number plate had found its way there. 'C'mon, give it to me.' On this instruction, William removed the plate from under his jacket and dutifully offered it to the policeman. As the officer grasped one end, William turned around and was off in a flash, leaving Arthur and me carrying the can (or in this case the number plate). Our policeman was plump and out of condition, so I was quite confident of being able to outrun him – but I hesitated for a second and that was my undoing. As I moved to escape there was just time enough for him to grab my shoulder. He might not have been built for sprinting, but there was certainly nothing wrong with his grip and in the ensuing brief struggle my shirtsleeve tore. It was my favourite corduroy shirt which was not only warm but also proved to be very strong. No matter how much I struggled, the sleeve remained firmly connected to the shirt and thus I remained inextricably attached to the policeman.

Arthur seemed to have already accepted that this was a fair cop and made no attempt to escape. With our captor grasping our upper arms firmly, we were duly marched off to a nearby police station, where the off-duty constable handed us over to a bored-looking desk sergeant.

'Okay, lads, you know the charge. It's theft of a number plate.' And then in a bored voice he formally cautioned us. 'You were caught red-handed. What d'you have to say?' There was little point in denying this, as the arresting officer, unseen to us, had observed the whole proceedings.

'Okay, so you admit to stealing the number-plate. Name and address, please?' He held a pencil poised over the sheet of paper on the desk in front of him. In a brief moment when we could talk without being overheard, Arthur and I had decided it would be best to say that we were unemployed and of no fixed abode, in an attempt to avoid being identified and so facing further possible sanctions from the University.

We gave our names. 'Addresses please?'

'No fixed abode.' Arthur was the first to reply. On saying this, the desk officer looked up at him unbelievingly, with a look that said, 'I know full well that you're a student and that you probably live in one of the nearby halls of residence.'

He turned his tired gaze on me. 'I suppose *you've* got no fixed abode as well?' I simply nodded. He didn't press us further but with a deep sigh scribbled our responses down on the paper in front of him.

'Right then, are you going to tell me the name of your friend who ran off?' The policeman looked up at Arthur and myself who remained silent. 'I'll take that as, a no, then,' and resumed his writing. We were asked to empty our pockets, the contents of which were placed in a brown paper bag, and then to remove our belts, which we duly handed over. Both of us were given a receipt before signing a form acknowledging that we had been duly cautioned.

Wearily, the policeman looked from Arthur to me. 'As you have both stated that you've no place of abode, you will have to remain in custody overnight, and appear at the Magistrates Court tomorrow.'

'But we've got...' Arthur was about to remonstrate and explain that we had lectures to attend the following day, but just in time thought better of it.

The policeman raised his eyebrows, 'Yes?'

'No, nothing.' Arthur's voice faded and his gaze turned to the floor.

'Okay. Off you go then.' So saying the policeman looked down, pencil in hand and began the process of completing his paperwork.

Thereafter, we were led down a corridor to the holding cells where Arthur and I were separated. I was ushered into one of the cells, the door being slammed and locked behind me. Once my eyes grew accustomed the semi-darkness, I was able to see a slatted bench running down either side of the room and a crude toilet at the far end. Sitting quietly to my left was a man of about fifty, wearing a dirty flat cap. I sat down opposite and surreptitiously examined my fellow-prisoner. He had a ruddy, outdoor complexion together with a broken nose, and was wearing working clothes. From under his cap tufts of greyish hair sprouted.

'Wot they got *you* for?' he asked, in a classic London working-class accent of the kind which would now be considered quite trendy. By now I was sobering up and the seriousness of the situation was sinking in.

'Stealing a car number plate.' I replied.

There was a long pause while my cell-mate gave due consideration to this reply. 'Deal in cars, d'you?'

'No.'

'Well wot d'you want to do that for?' he asked with a genuinely surprised look on his face.

It was a good question. The fact that it would have looked good above William's ONE WAY sign now hardly seemed credible.

'God alone knows,' I replied.

'Well,' continued my companion, 'they picked *me* up just 'cos I *look* like a villain.' He paused, while I registered surprise at discovering that you could be arrested for just resembling a criminal. 'I was going up me own path. Nearly inside me 'ouse I was. At the front door. I done nothing wrong – not an effing fing! The rozzers always picks me up just 'cos I looks like a villain,' my cellmate moaned. He was right though – there was no doubting the fact that he did look the real McCoy; a genuine villain.

'Too stupid. That's me. Too stupid' he went on. 'I'm a labourer, I am. I does what I'm told. I dig 'oles. If the gaffer says, "Dig a 'ole," I digs a 'ole. If he says, "Dig arf a 'ole," I digs arf a 'ole.'

I had to agree that he did indeed seem to have had a stroke of bad luck and after an in-depth discussion about the unfairness of life in general – and for the two of us in particular – I managed to bring our conversation to a close. My new friend quickly fell asleep and started to snore loudly, while my mind went wild with the possibilities of what might happen. A jail sentence maybe: and how many years would I get? Time off for good behaviour? Good job the death penalty had been abolished, I thought. In the small hours of the night, the more I let my mind wander, the worse my situation seemed. I tried to get some sleep but with little success.

Just a few hours later the cell became lighter and there was a rattle of keys in the lock. A cheery warden entered. 'Morning all! It's a beautiful day outside. Here, have some breakfast,' and so saying he laid two mugs and two plates on the bench near the door.

'Thanks,' I said, picking up a buttered roll and a mug of indeterminate warm fluid. As the warden closed and locked the door behind him, I turned to my new friend and, looking at the roll, said, 'Not much of a breakfast. Hardly a repast for the gods.'

'Wot for the gods?'

'Feast. Not much to eat.' I clarified.

'Oh! I don't know; better than last time,' he replied knowledgably, slurping down the last of his tea. 'Not like the ol' days though; used to get a cooked breakfast. Luvely that was.'

A few minutes later the door was again unlocked and we were escorted the short distance to a courtyard at the rear of the police station, where there was parked a Black-Maria, its engine running. We were ushered inside and there, looking down at his desert boots, was Arthur, seated at the front of the van and squashed between two large prisoners. I sat down nearby and nodded. 'Sleep well?' I asked ironically.

He looked up, and after a brief smile of recognition, glumly replied, 'Not a wink.' He was about to elaborate when the warden, who had just closed the doors at the rear of the van, sat down with us, and barked loudly, 'No talking.'

We all fell silent and, after being jostled around for what seemed an age, arrived at the court. We waited in a poorly-lit basement holding-cell until our names were called, when one by one were escorted into the courtroom. Eventually it was our turn.

'Mr Howard and Mr Wilkinson, please.' Arthur and I stood and were taken up a steep flight of stone stairs. Following a brief halt on a landing at the top, a wooden door was flung open and sunlight flooded into the stairwell. Suddenly we found ourselves standing in the dock, nervously blinking in the bright courtroom. In front of us, on the opposite side of the room and seated on the bench, was a man in a pinstriped suit whom we assumed was the magistrate. Between him and us, in the well of the court, were various gowned figures behind their desks, surrounded by books and papers. The pair of us stood there together looking pathetic, I imagine, rather than villainous. In addition to my tattered shirt, the absence of a belt meant that my trousers had a tendency to slip down. I therefore had to alternate between tugging at my sleeve and pulling up my trousers to maintain any sort of dignity and retain some semblance of sartorial normality.

One of the gowned clerks came and stood in front of us and asked, 'Would you state your names and addresses, please?' Arthur and I gave our names and said that we were of no fixed abode. All eyes then turned to the magistrate who was perusing some papers on the desk in front of him. At length, he looked up, peering over the tortoiseshell frame of his half-moon glasses.

'You are charged with the theft of a number plate. How do you plead?

'Guilty,' we replied.

'You state you are of no fixed abode, and unemployed. Do you expect me to believe that?' We said nothing.

'As you choose not to answer, tell me – *if* you will – where did you go to school?' I responded first and then Arthur gave the name of his famous public school. A quiet titter could be heard emanating from the well of the court. 'Although you may be unemployed I find it difficult to believe that you have no place of abode. I ask you both again, where do you live?' Arthur and I looked at each other, and without a word agreed that we should tell the truth.

Arthur said, 'Liverpool Hall, – a hall of residence in Cartwright Gardens.'

'And you?'

'The same.' I replied.

'You live in a London University hall of residence so one must assume that you are students. Tell me, *if* you would, what you are studying?'

'Medicine,' I replied growing increasingly upset in the face of this unsympathetic questioning.

The magistrate removed his glasses and placed them on the desk. 'You have had a privileged education and are studying to enter one of the most respected of professions and yet you perpetrate this crass act which could ruin your whole future. You deserve to be taught a lesson.'

My head was sinking lower still and I feared the worst. A custodial sentence would mean expulsion from St Thomas' and a premature end to what was already proving to be a rather unpromising career. I glanced at Arthur whose face was deathly white.

'What do you have to say for yourselves?' asked the magistrate with an air of finality.

As we began to apologise profusely, one of the clerks presented the magistrate with a note. Arthur and I continued to grovel our apologies and I took the opportunity to haul my trousers up once again. After having read the note with great care, the magistrate looked up. 'All right, all right. That's enough! You may stop there.' We ceased apologising and stared at the floor of the dock in silence.

He then continued: 'As it happens, I am now informed that the car involved in this incident was one which our police have been seeking for some months and the number plates were false. The vehicle contained a significant amount of stolen goods.' The magistrate paused. 'I find myself placed in a difficult position. Whilst I abhor your behaviour and feel you deserve to be punished severely, you have – albeit quite inadvertently – helped the police to recover stolen property.' He paused again and looked towards the clerks of the court. 'I need to take advice.' The magistrate then conversed with two of the clerks while Arthur and I looked at each other, quite mystified, having no idea of what might happen. After a few minutes he looked up.

'Mr Howard and Mr Wilkinson, as you have apologised for your misdemeanour and have – albeit unwittingly – aided the police in the recovery of stolen goods, I am inclined in this exceptional circumstance to be lenient. You are each fined ten pounds, to be paid within thirty days. Do you have anything to say?'

'No, sir.' Arthur and I responded in unison.

'Gentlemen, you are free to go.'

We thanked the magistrate and with audible sighs of relief left the dock as quickly as possible, before the magistrate could change his mind. We were escorted to the main entrance to the court, where we were given back our belongings and, with our trousers now tightly secured again, the door was opened. Once back in the fresh air, we began to run down the street, slowly at first and then as fast as we could. We sprinted for about a hundred yards before we stopped to catch breath. As we did so, we instinctively looked back to confirm that we weren't being followed. We couldn't believe our luck, although I wasn't at all sure where I would find the ten pounds to pay the fine.

Arthur and I didn't return directly to our hall as we still absurdly imagined that someone might be tailing us, so we took a detour and then, satisfied that we were not being followed, went to see William. We took the escalator to the fifth floor and walked along the corridor to his room where I knocked loudly on the door. William meanwhile, had been in a state of panic all night expecting a visit from the constabulary. From inside the room came a faint strangled voice and in a strange accent – Scottish with a hint of German – we heard, 'Aye. Who is zere?' spoken slowly and with a distinctly public school accent.

I knocked again more loudly. This time there was a touch of the oriental. 'Dinne ken. No understandee,' came the response.

By now Arthur had suffered quite enough of this nonsense. 'William! Open up, you damned fool. It's only us,' he shouted.

The door opened a fraction and William's blanched face appeared. His eyes were red, his hair dishevelled and he was still in his pyjamas, but with a cravat around his neck. He peered cautiously through the crack in the door. Once he was satisfied that we were indeed who we claimed to be, he emerged into the corridor, closing the door behind him and looking up and down its entire length to be sure we were quite alone. He then hustled us into his room, closing and locking the door securely behind him.

'Are you *absolutely* sure you haven't been followed?' he whispered, having now dropped his phoney accents.

William was ashen-faced and clearly hadn't slept a wink. His room looked different too. All the spoils of numerous nights out – including his prized ONE WAY ONLY sign – were nowhere to be seen.

'Where have you two *been*?' He was still whispering but now more audibly and urgently.

'Where d'you think? You *idiot*!' Arthur was in no mood for mincing words. '*In jail*.'

I then added, rather melodramatically, 'We did *time* for you.'

'I didn't know what to do. I thought you might tell them where I lived and they'd come after me. I spent the whole night taking all the signs down to an empty cellar in Sandwich Street.' William had been pacing about the room but now sat down and put his head in his hands.

'We didn't tell them who you were. Eventually we admitted to living in Liverpool Hall, but there's no way they can trace you.'

'Are you *sure*?'

'Yes. Absolutely.' Arthur and I continued to reassure William and after some time he began to calm down.

'Well. Thanks, chaps. I appreciate that.'

Although reassured to some degree, it was to be many weeks before William stopped worrying that the police might suddenly arrive to arrest him and, needless to say, we abandoned our souvenir-collecting – for a while at least. I decided to concentrate on trying to attract a member of the opposite sex, with a view – as the adverts say – to friendship, fun and possibly more.

CHAPTER 4:

MYOPIA AND A MISMATCH

After the little unpleasantness of the car number plate incident, we determined to remain firmly on the right side of the law and lead exemplary studious lives. Indeed, life in Liverpool Hall was pleasant. There were squash courts for the athletic and the basement housed a grand piano on which I would play from time to time. Something, however, was missing, and that something was my continuing failure to attract a girl with whom I could lose my virginity. I was reassured by the fact that many of my friends seemed as sexually inexperienced as I was.

Justin, who was a veterinary student, lived three rooms along the corridor from me and one night as I passed his door, which was slightly ajar, he popped his head out. 'Psst! Grahame, do you want to come and have a look?'

'Look at what?'

'A naked woman!'

'A what?'

'A naked woman! You know, a woman – but with no clothes on.'

'What! In your room?' I was intrigued.

'No, you idiot. Come in and have a look, but don't open the door too much or you'll ruin our night vision.' So saying, he opened the door a little further and I entered his room, which was in complete darkness. Inside were six or seven other students, one of whom was peering through a telescope set up at the open window, trained upon a hotel room on the opposite side of the gardens.

'Stewart thought he saw a naked women a moment ago.' Justin said this quietly as though he were in a hide delivering the commentary for a wildlife documentary. 'Here, let me have a look,' he whispered as he nudged Stewart away from the telescope and put his own eye to it. 'Yes! Yes! I can see something. I think it's an arm.' Justin was getting excited. 'Yes. Yes, it's definitely an arm. She's lifting her arm. She's . . . Oh bugger! She's closed the curtains.' Justin lifted his head from the eyepiece of the telescope, switched the room lights on and said, 'Sorry, chaps. That's it: end of tonight's entertainment.'

* * *

'I see you've still not opened your pack of three, then,' said William as he observed the unmistakable oval shape etched into the surface of my wallet. A group of us, including William and Arthur, were in The Norfolk Arms just behind Cartwright Gardens for an early evening beer or two and I had taken out my wallet to buy a round of drinks.

'Actually, I've had a bit of luck on the old bedroom front and this is a new packet,' I lied without conviction.

'Bollocks! It's your glasses. They're a real turn-off for women. You should get some contact lenses like me.' William had made a number of adjustments to his appearance since we had first met. His hair was longer, the cravat and cavalry twill had been replaced by a T-shirt and jeans; and he now wore contact lenses nearly all the time.

'Have *you* pulled then?'

'Well – no! Not exactly.' William faltered slightly. 'Not technically – in the *strictest* sense.' He then grew more assertive. 'But at least *I* can differentiate between men and women and can recognise which girl I'm supposed to be dancing with.' William was referring to an unfortunate incident, which had occurred directly as a result of my short-sightedness.

For those of us who misguidedly thought that by removing our spectacles we would instantly become irresistible to the opposite sex, there were a limited number of options. One of these was to remove our glasses when in the presence of women. This could be risky for the severely myopic, as there was a very real danger of accidents. Above-ground hazards included other human beings and lamp posts; and then there were large holes such as road-works or stairwells, all of which, if unseen, could result in serious injury. William, however, was referring to the occasion when, having removed my glasses to ask a girl for a dance, I failed to identify her again when I came back from a visit to the Gents. After criss-crossing the dance floor for some time, I thought I recognised her and started to gyrate in that jerky uncoordinated fashion that I called dancing – only to find, on closer inspection, that I was now dancing with a rather surprised, long-haired man. I still suspect that the girl in question took the opportunity of my needing a comfort break to escape from the embarrassment of being associated with someone who danced like an oversized Flower-Pot Man.

Charles – who had been party to this conversation – was in our year and stayed in the same hall of residence as William. He was good company, friendly and generous, but even his mother couldn't have called him handsome. He was short and plump, had spots, large tomb-stone teeth and obstinately maintained the cravat and tweed jacket dress-style. However, as far as he was concerned, his glasses were the only hindrance to his being irresistible to women of all ages. It's true his spectacles had those thick black frames made popular by Buddy Holly some twenty years before, and the lenses were of a thickness that made the wearer look as though he had very small, pig-like eyes. Charles however, actually did have small, pig-like eyes.

Some weeks later, while walking along Cartwright Gardens one morning, I spotted Charles coming towards me. He looked rather strange but I wasn't sure quite why. As he narrowly missed a lamp post, I could see that he was crying, yet he seemed to be smiling at the same time. He was smoking his pipe and I thought a puff of wind must have blown the smoke into his eyes. As he came closer and walked into a MEN AT WORK sign, nearly knocking it over, I realised why he looked different – he wasn't wearing his spectacles. Once he reached me, I could see his eyes were bright red and that tears were streaming down his cheeks. After narrowly avoiding a cyclist, and then peering unseeingly in my direction for some time, he eventually recognised me, and exclaimed with a broad smile, 'Wonderful things these contact lenses! Now I've got them I shouldn't have any problems attracting the opposite sex!'

I didn't like to disabuse him of this new-found confidence. 'Absolutely, Charles,' I agreed. 'Aren't they a just a *trifle* uncomfortable though?' I said hesitantly.

'Oh yes! They hurt like buggery at the moment, but the girl in the shop said that this initial slight discomfort will soon wear off.'

'Couldn't help noticing that you nearly walked into a quite a few things as well,' I remarked casually as though this was of little significance.

'Oh, that's just the acute reaction. Obviously I can barely see anything at all *now,* but the girl says that my sight will soon improve. Nice girl! She said she thought they suited me and that I looked rather handsome without my glasses.' Charles began to smile at the memory, but in so doing set off a spasm of pain, causing a fresh flood of tears to cascade down his face.

I could only congratulate him on his brilliant transformation. After helping him across the road and pointing him in the direction of his hall of residence, I walked on, only to hear another yell of pain as he completely misjudged the steps up to the entrance – thinking they were about three feet nearer than they actually were – and fell flat on his face, grazing himself quite badly.

* * *

Saturdays during term time were dedicated to sport, which in our early years at St Thomas' meant rugby. St Thomas' possessed a wonderful sports ground and pavilion south of London in leafy Cobham. A bunch of us from the first year formed what was in effect a fourth XV. Fixtures were fairly hit-or-miss affairs, with some proving to be a complete mismatch. At times we would be trounced, occasionally we actually won, while sometimes the opposition wouldn't even show up.

It was a home game at Cobham and the St Thomas' Fourths were all togged up and ready, milling around the changing rooms or punting a ball about the pitch. We were a truly motley crew and had only scraped a team together by enlisting two soccer players who had never played rugger before. While William was giving them some last-minute tuition, reassuring them that it really was permissible to pick the ball up and run with it, other members of the team lounged about on the sidelines, smoking and chatting quietly. Charles, who was playing at number eight, was smoking his pipe while trying to get his contact lenses to stay in place. The kick-off time of 2.30 p.m. came and went with no sign of the opposing team, and at 3 o'clock they still hadn't arrived.

'Well, I don't think they're coming. I'm heading for the bar. Anyone want to join me?' William announced while unlacing his boots.

'Good idea,' I said, following suit. Soon the whole team was in the bar and we were on our third pint when I managed to engage in what I thought was a promising conversation with a student nurse who had come along to support us. It was after 3.30 and the light was beginning to fail when a small coach pulled up in the car park outside.

'God! I hope that's not them,' William said, as clearly we were by now expecting a no-show. However, sadly it was indeed the opposing team and less than a minute later an athletic-looking, fresh-faced young stockbroker appeared in the doorway. He put his bag on the floor and walked over to the bar where we were standing. He looked all around casually, and then, addressing no one in particular announced: 'Hi, chaps. I'm Andy, captain of the Investors' Fifteen and we're here to play Tommies' Fourths. Awfully sorry we're late, but we got caught up in some horrendous traffic in south London. Some sort of demonstration, apparently. Who's your captain?'

William detached himself from the bar and pint in hand went over to introduce himself. 'We rather thought that you weren't coming and so we've abandoned the game. Would you like a beer?'

'Oh! rather not. Surely we can still have our match? My chaps are just getting changed, and they're terribly keen to have a game. Never played a hospital side before.'

I wandered over and whispered into William's ear. 'I think we should cancel it, William. We're in no fit state to play. Look, Steve can barely stand.' I nodded towards our winger, one of our star players, who was swaying dangerously beside the bar, his eyes glazed and unfocussed. It was growing cold outside, while by now I was on my fourth pint and felt I was making real progress with the nurse, whose name I had ascertained was Susan. I emptied my glass. 'Anyone for another?' I asked looking at the motley crew that comprised Tommies' Fourths. As I said this, I could see the rest of the Investors' XV running athletically out on to the pitch. Once there, they warmed up with star jumps, and bunny hops – jumping, stretching, slapping each other on the back and generally behaving like complete pains in the arse.

'Oh, no!' I groaned. William did his best but Andy wouldn't take no for an answer and eventually we felt obliged to put our boots back on and join the visitors in the deepening gloom of that late autumn afternoon.

There were one or two supporters on the touchline, including Susan whom I had been trying to impress in the bar. A few minutes after kick-off I saw my first piece of the action. I was playing at full back and a high ball sailed towards me. There was plenty of time to catch it as the opposition forwards were still a good thirty yards away so I stationed myself underneath the ball, arms in the correct cradle-catching position, and watched with amazement as it hit the ground and bounced some two yards to my left. I retrieved the ball with a view to a stylish kick into touch. Clearly my hand, eye and foot co-ordination had been adversely affected by the pre-match drinks. I tossed the ball forward and extended my foot for the kick. Not only did I miss the ball by a mile, but having one foot off the ground had completely destabilised me and I fell over. This happened a second time and only at the third attempt did I manage to connect with the ball, successfully dispatching it into touch.

I heard Susan scream, 'Well done! Good kick! *Come on, Tommies.*' Luckily she knew nothing at all about the game but her support encouraged me and I ran athletically back to my position, trying to look as much like JPR Williams as I could while pretending that missing the catch, then the kick, and finally falling over, all formed part of some elaborate game-plan. Unfortunately, all those exertions were now making me decidedly nauseous and so, after unsuccessfully trying to rectify the situation by taking several deep breaths, I gave up and ran to the sideline where I threw up, not yards from my solitary admirer. I wasn't the only one having problems, however. Charles lost one of his contact lenses during his first skirmish with the opposition forwards and the game had to be suspended for the best part of fifteen minutes while both teams walked along the pitch, line abreast, eyes down, searching for it. Amazingly it was found and the game continued, for a while at least. I am uncertain how long the referee allowed the agony to continue, but I seem to recall the game was abandoned after less than an hour (including the time spent locating the contact lens) when it became clear that our position as the losing team was firmly and quite irrevocably established.

After the match, as was customary, we entertained the visiting team with drinks and a meal. Because of the game's curtailment we had around four hours of drinking time before the bar closed.

Even imbibing at a modest pace this allowed for almost a gallon of beer to be consumed before embarking on the trip home. The only drawback to visiting Cobham was the return journey to London. None of us at that time had a car, which was a just as well since as after a game we were never in a fit state to drive, but it did mean taking the train from Cobham Station back to Waterloo. The opposing team had long since departed when Arthur, William and I finished our final drinks and left the sports pavilion for home. We were relieved to reach the station just in time to board the last train, for the forty-five minute journey to Waterloo Station.

Those commuter trains had no corridors and so we were confined to our carriage for the duration of the journey without access to a toilet. Even having taken the precaution of relieving ourselves at the last possible opportunity while crossing the playing fields, I could sense my own bladder filling up the moment our train had pulled out of Cobham Station. I held out stoically for some considerable time before finally accepting that I would have to relieve myself before we reached London and that this would inevitably involve the tricky and slightly dangerous manoeuvre of urinating out of the train window. Each carriage door had a window, which in those days could be lowered by means of a leather strap. Fixed to the door below the window was a small brass knob, which enabled the belt-like strap to secure the window in the desired position.

After announcing my intention to Arthur and William – luckily there were no other passengers in that particular carriage – I lowered the window into the carriage door as far as it would go. However, this was still not low enough so I clambered on to the seat where I half-stood and half-wedged myself in a precarious position from where I could just raise my penis over the glass. Psychologically, this was not the ideal position for initiating urination and it took a while for the flow to begin but, once started, it went from strength to strength and the relief was immeasurable. It was decidedly unfortunate that the train simultaneously started to slow on approaching a station.

'For God's sake, Grahame, get down, we're coming to a station!' Arthur was becoming concerned that my behaviour might result in another altercation with the law and yet a further court appearance.

'I can't. I'm not finished,' I moaned.

'It's okay, Arthur. Calm down. This train doesn't stop here.' William was correct, in that the train was not scheduled to stop, but nevertheless it slowed to little more than walking pace and in the dusk I could see the lights of the station approaching and a surprising number of commuters standing on the platform, waiting for the next train. I tried to stop, but couldn't, for a gallon of beer builds up a lot of pressure and once the dam was breached there was no staunching the flow. I had no choice but to let nature take its course and could only avert my eyes in shame as the train passed slowly through the station.

CHAPTER 5:

THE GLASS EYE AND THE MORTUARY TROLLEY

I spent many agreeable hours in the anatomy room dissecting my way around the human body. It was not dissimilar to my schoolboy dissection of a rat, but of course on a much larger scale. Our team was an eclectic mix of very different personalities. Eddie's ambition was to follow in his father's footsteps and become a general practitioner, preferably in north London which was his home. He still lapsed into Derek Guyler mode in moments of stress and occasionally we would hear, 'I was in the Desert Rats, y'know,' emanating from our cadaver while he was dissecting. Then there was Mike – short in stature, blond and good-looking – who always seemed to be one step ahead of the rest of us, whether it was in general worldliness and life experience, such as sex and dress sense, or indeed in our academic studies. He had a long-term girlfriend who was a model and, unlike most of us, Mike had completed the transition from pubescent desire and frustration to a fulfilling sexual relationship.

Pete also had long fair hair, but instead of falling as gentle shiny waves in a Greek god-like fashion, it was coarse and frizzy, sticking out perpendicular to his head and making him look a bit like a surprised sunflower. It didn't help that he had embraced the dress style of the sixties in its entirety without any recourse to good taste. He wore hipsters with a wide belt, a striped shirt with a kipper tie, and his Cuban heeled shoes elevated him to a height of about six feet. Pete was the only one of us from a comprehensive school – which caused him to have something of a chip on his shoulder. This was usually well-disguised but would occasionally manifest itself through his acerbic wit. Not so long ago, St Thomas' students had all come from public schools and wore (it was said) bowler hats and a suit during dissection, out of respect for the dead. The hat rule was subsequently abandoned and grammar school boys were admitted, but suits were still mandatory. More recently, the dress code had been relaxed completely and St Thomas' now accepted students from all educational backgrounds, provided they were academically qualified. Pete was aware that he was in the vanguard of this new movement. As for me – as Rupert Brooke described himself – I was something of a chameleon. I could become whatever people demanded of me. In sporty company, I was slightly athletic; with musicians I became musical; and with thinkers I turned philosophical. I tried to combine the romantic aura of Lord Byron with the epigrammatic wit of Oscar Wilde. This was fairly difficult while owning only one pair of denim jeans, a few old school shirts, and an ancient Paisley-patterned cravat.

After dissecting the upper and lower limbs, we moved on to the head and neck. It was only then that we found our corpse possessed a glass eye. Once carefully cleansed, this proved to be a pleasant trinket and a potential solution to one of my perennial problems – somnolence during lectures. For me, biochemistry was by far the most soporific of all the subjects we studied. I would generally start to yawn and my eyes droop even as we approached the lecture theatre, only to fall sound asleep within five minutes of a lecture starting. Falling asleep *per se* was not necessarily the main problem – most lecturers expect a few members of their class to be asleep and learn to ignore them – but waking up could be fraught with problems. Dozing off is, of course, much more noticeable within smaller groups, such as tutorials, where one individual being sound asleep is difficult to ignore. In later life I had a friend who managed to fall asleep in a one-to-one tutorial.

In his defence, I should explain that the subject was physics, probably for many the most somniferous topic in the universe. Even now, if I ever find it difficult to get to sleep – a very rare problem for me – I simply have to open a physics textbook, start to read and usually doze off before I have completed the first sentence. In fact I think the NHS could save an enormous amount in costs if doctors simply issued insomniacs with a physics primer rather than by prescribing tablets. To return to my friend: on this occasion, after manfully trying to keep his eyes open for about ten minutes, he finally gave up the struggle, let his eyelids close and drifted into the arms of Morpheus. A while later he briefly awoke from his dreams and looked up, only to find the lecturer seated opposite him, head on his arms, sound asleep and snoring quietly.

As I have already expounded, it is not necessarily the status of being asleep, but the events which may occur as a result of that somnolent condition, which can prove disruptive. Noisy snoring may irritate the rest of the class, and nightmares *may* be disruptive, but the process of waking can be much more disturbing as it generally involves some form of startle reaction. Normally, when you wake up at home it's in your own bed in the predictable and comforting surroundings of one's own bedroom, and the whole process is gradual and pleasant. During a lecture the situation is entirely different because, instead of finding yourself in the cosy, friendly environment of your own bedroom, the surroundings now seem unfamiliar. You find that your bedroom has unexpectedly become transformed into a packed lecture theatre, and that everyone is staring at you. This all happens in a nano-second after which the ghastly truth dawns upon you and you do the least sensible thing possible – suddenly sit bolt upright and deliver a loud yell. *That* is the startle reaction. If that is not sufficient to draw attention to yourself, the whole process is usually accompanied by vigorous and uncontrolled arm-waving, sufficient to cause minor injury to one's neighbours and to dislodge any nearby items such as books and pens. It is those events that lead the lecturer to infer that you have just awoken from a deep sleep. Some years later, when a junior doctor, this happened to me when my pager went off while I was sound asleep during a seminar. As well as the predictable startle reaction, which was disruptive enough, I succeeded, during a moment of post-somnolent disorientation, in entering a large cupboard, in the mistaken belief that it was the exit. Sadly this was not the end to this debacle as I then had to cross the breadth of the room, in front of the projection screen, to reach the real exit. Somehow during this process my foot became entangled with the tripod supporting the screen, which them fell forward, narrowly missing those in the front row and dislodging the projector from its stand. The resulting confusion was such that our guest speaker never truly recovered his composure.

The glass eye, I thought, could be the solution. Such an object is not spherical, as you might imagine, but dish-shaped and I discovered that it could be conveniently inserted over my own closed eye – thus giving the impression of being alert and attentive while actually being fast asleep. At least that was the idea. I determined to try this out during the next biochemistry lecture. Sadly, like so many of my plans, it had one or two slight flaws. Firstly, I had only a single glass eye, so it appeared as if I was winking at the lecturer; and secondly, as it didn't fit snugly into the eye socket, it gave me a sort of staring appearance as though I was thyrotoxic or at best leering at the lecturer in a salacious, one-eyed fashion. The other problem was that, as I fell asleep, my orbicularis oculi muscle – that is, the one around my eye that I was relying on to keep the glass eye in place – would relax, resulting in the glass eye falling out on to the bench in front of me with a surprisingly loud tinkling noise. This naturally resulted in the invariable startle reaction. As I picked up my books and searched for my missing eye, the professor of biochemistry who was delivering the lecture broke off from his enthralling description of the Krebbs cycle to say, 'Mr. Howard, I think one of your eyes has fallen out. Kindly stay awake.' This was followed by howls of laughter from the rest of the class, which echoed around the lecture theatre for some time to my discomfiture.

* * *

My first year as a medical student was followed by a lengthy summer holiday. Back in Norwich, I signed on as a porter at the West Norwich Hospital in order to earn enough money to pay off my rapidly accruing debts and perhaps even to fund a holiday. Finding casual labour in the seventies was much easier than it is now. I had worked as a porter at the West Norwich during school holidays in the past and I simply pitched up at the porters' lodge, saw Sandy, the Glaswegian head porter, and asked if he had any jobs. When he announced he had a vacancy, we agreed that I should start work the following Monday.

As well as Sandy, there was another familiar face from previous summers. Ernie looked about eighty, was tall and thin with a forward stoop, and possessed a gaunt face which featured a large hooked nose decorated with a maze of tiny blue veins. His head bore a few long strands of grey hair which he would endeavour to keep in place on top of his otherwise bald pate. He had enormous feet which were ensconced in still larger, tatty, black, scuffed leather shoes. Ernie always looked cold, even on the hottest of summer days. After being issued with my porter's brown, knee-length coat, I was introduced to two new faces. The first was a young man in his early twenties who was quite short and slightly overweight, wearing well-polished black shoes with steel tips which persistently made an annoying clicking noise whenever he walked. It turned out that he had been educated at Harrow and was between what he called 'proper' jobs. The second was a tall, thin, untrustworthy-looking character who was later convicted of the theft of a purse at a nurses' party.

Porters were the lowest members of the hospital food chain and so were considered to be legitimate targets for abuse from all other ranks of hospital employee. The chefs would yell at me for delivering or not delivering the food trolleys. I was always too late, too early, too fast, too slow, too *something*. Whenever I entered the slippery, greasy environment of the kitchen, a tirade of insults, directed at me, would emanate from the head chef, and all the other chefs would laugh loudly at my expense. As well as delivering food trolleys, we porters transported anything and everything, including, of course, patients.

Sandy had a little cubbyhole in the corner of the porters' lodge. Here, from behind a wooden counter, he could answer the phone and observe the entrance to the hospital. One week into my stint, I was sitting chatting to him when he took a call and said, 'Grahame, would you go and fetch Mrs Williams from Ward 12 and take her to X-ray?' Obediently, I grabbed a wheelchair from outside the porter's lodge and headed straight for Ward 12. This was on the first floor and it was only few minutes later that I trundled the chair into the ward to seek out a nurse. Seated at a desk with her back towards me was the ward sister, her head bent over the report she was writing. As I approached I could see tiny wisps of hair on the nape of her neck which had not been caught up in the tight bun she was wearing, and I detected a delicate flowery smell of perfume.

'Excuse me.' As I said this, she turned and looked up at me. She was young and slim, her pretty face enhanced by a hint of make-up. Her cheeks were a delicate, opaque blush of pink; her eyes, beneath jet-black brows, were dark and piercing; and her lips were an exuberant red. This alluring picture was framed by dark, auburn hair swept back very tightly beneath her immaculate white linen cap. I started to blush and made an attempt to smile. 'I've come to take Mrs Williams to X-ray.'

As soon as she heard this, her demeanour hardened. 'You're late! It's almost dinner time.'

'Sorry,' I stammered.

'Just make sure you bring her back within half an hour or else she'll miss her meal.' Her expression was icy, but this in no way detracted from her beauty and simply made her seem all the more desirable.

'She's down there on the left – third bed from the end,' she said tersely, before turning to resume her writing. I pushed the wheelchair down the ward towards an elderly, thin, grey-haired lady who sat dozing in an armchair beside her bed. Her wrinkled, light-brown stockings were halfway down her shrunken legs and there were stains of spilled food in the lap of her black dress.

'Mrs Williams?' I asked. There was no answer and all I could hear was a high-pitched whine from her hearing aid. I tried again, louder this time along with a gentle shake of her shoulder: 'I've come to take you to X-ray.' Eventually she awoke and, with the correct patient in the chair, it was back along the corridor, down the rickety lift and along the ground floor corridor to X-ray, the whole process taking less than twenty minutes. I parked the chair in the X-ray reception area and with a bright smile announced cheerily, 'This is Mrs Williams from ward 12.'

The receptionist was middle-aged, with thickly powdered wrinkled cheeks and light gingery-brown hair, greying near the roots. Her pink-framed spectacles dangled from a chain around her neck and lay upon her ample bosom. She looked up angrily. 'Where *have* you been? She was supposed to be here an hour ago.'

'I'm so sorry. But I brought her along as soon as I was asked.'

She was not to be mollified. 'And where are her X-rays? Don't tell me you haven't brought them.'

'I'm sorry. I didn't know.' I was now growing extremely flustered. 'Shall I go and fetch them? It'll only take two minutes.'

'They're supposed to come with her.' She let out a deep sigh. 'You should know that. You porters are hopeless! I asked for her to be sent down at ten o'clock and it's now eleven-thirty. That's just *not* good enough. She'll just have to go back.'

Things were not going well and, as the receptionist was growing increasingly ill-tempered, I began to feel correspondingly embarrassed and uneasy. Several outpatients sitting in the waiting area were eagerly following this altercation and seemed to be siding with the receptionist.

'Should have brought the X-rays, son,' said one old man in a sports jacket with a trilby hat perched at a jaunty angle on his head. 'Everyone knows that.'

''E's only young. Give 'im a chance. 'E's got to learn,' interposed a middle-aged, wheezy lady in a brightly-coloured floral dress who seemed to be siding with me.

The receptionist continued her tirade. 'These porters are all idiots, *and* they get paid nearly as much as me!' This was directed at the flowery, wheezy lady. Things were generally getting somewhat out of hand when a radiographer bustled out of the X-ray room and looked at me angrily.

'*Don't tell me* that's Mrs Williams!'

Just for a moment I considered lying and saying, 'No, this is *not* Mrs Williams' – but then thought better of it. Instead I meekly apologised. 'Sorry.'

'This is my break, you know!' continued the radiographer snatching the notes and request card from my hand. 'Oh, I suppose I'd better . . .' The sentence was left unfinished as she angrily seized the chair from me. To this day I swear I heard a clucking noise as she disappeared into the darkened interior of the X-ray room. Throughout all this, Mrs Williams dozed quietly, occasionally lifting her head and smiling benignly, her hearing aid whining away gently in the background.

My humiliation wasn't yet complete. By the time her X-ray was taken and I had wheeled Mrs Williams back to the ward, I had been away for nearly an hour. As I pushed the chair into the ward the pretty nurse glowered at me. 'What on *earth* took you so long? Her dinner's getting cold.' I didn't even try to explain.

'Sorry.' I mumbled, blushing deeply.

Interestingly, after a few weeks I noticed that the X-ray receptionist, the radiographer and even some of the nurses had become much more friendly towards me. I shared this observation with Sandy.

'Aye, that'll be 'cos they ken ye're a medical student now, and nae just a bluidy porter,' he commented quietly.

* * *

We had all been summoned to the porters' lodge, which was situated on the left of the entrance to the hospital, near the main road – aptly named Waterworks Road. To say that Ernie looked amazed would be an understatement. In his left hand was an open laundry bag, which smelt, as they always do, of urine. In his right hand was the arm of a wheelchair, which he had just removed from the bag. His eyes were wide with amazement, 'How's that got there?' He asked the question of himself as much as of the assembled audience.

'Fantastic! Fantastic!' was all that Sandy could say in his crisp Glaswegian accent. 'What *will* they think of next? You'd think someone would miss half a wheel-chair – how on earth has it got into a laundry bag?' He was lost for words and all he could do was mutter, 'Fantastic! That's fantastic.'

But the contents of the laundry bag were not the reason for Sandy calling this meeting. He was clearly stressed and annoyed, having received a complaint that his porters had been slow in delivering the cardiac arrest trolley to an emergency. After some investigation it was discovered that Ernie had been carrying the cardiac arrest pager at the time in question. Ernie was nearing retirement and consequently was not the fastest porter on two legs. Sandy confronted him with the evidence and asked why it had taken him so long to get the arrest trolley to the desired location.

'I thought that were a joke!' he replied in his broad Norwich accent.

On hearing this extraordinary statement, all of us turned and stared at Ernie in amazement.

'You thought it was a *joke!*' said Sandy, his voice growing louder. 'You thought it was a *joke?*'

'Yeah, I thought that were one of them jokes. One of them false alarms,' Ernie continued. 'But when I knew that weren't, I rushed.'

'But it took you *three-quarters of an hour*!' yelled an exasperated Sandy.

'I know, but I had to go across the road. It were right busy and I had to wait for the traffic. Then I had to stop half-way up the hill when my lace come undone and my shoe fell orf,' Ernie explained.

Ernie certainly had a valid point. The problem was that the hospital spanned both sides of Waterworks Road and the cardiac arrest had occurred in a ward on the opposite side. Not only had Ernie to wait for a gap in the traffic, but on the other side there was a steep incline up which it was very difficult to push a heavy trolley, even with both shoe laces firmly tied.

'Fantastic! Fantastic!' was all Sandy could say.

The mortuary was also sited on the other side of the road. Putting the recently deceased into the refrigerators was one of our many tasks. For excellent reasons, mortuaries are not usually situated in the busiest areas of a hospital. There was, however, at least one exception – at Bangour Hospital in West Lothian. There, somewhat disconcertingly, the mortuary was the first building a visitor saw on entering the hospital grounds just to the left of the main entrance and opposite the canteen. At the West Norwich, however, it was discreetly tucked away in the darkest and most secluded part of the grounds.

On the night shift, there were only two porters on duty for the whole hospital, and if one of them was otherwise engaged, delivering bodies had to be performed single-handedly. It was the following Friday night that I was called to take a body from Ward 12 to the mortuary. I was mildly excited, hoping that the delicious nurse I had met earlier on that week might again be there and I resolved not to give her any cause for complaint this time. Sadly she wasn't on duty, but there were two somewhat less pretty but decidedly more muscular nurses, which was lucky, as the corpse was of an eighteen-stone man. With some difficulty the three of us managed to lower the body into the mortuary trolley. This vehicle is a strange contraption, being designed to look like a normal trolley so that the uninitiated do not know there is a corpse inside. Basically, it *is* a normal trolley, but with a concealed compartment underneath into which the body is placed. It therefore looks rather like a coffin on wheels but when covered with a sheet the section containing the corpse is hidden. This artifice fools none but the most naïve.

Once loaded up, I wheeled the now extremely heavy trolley along the main hospital drive. I was concerned about pushing it up the incline on the other side of Waterworks Road so I parked it temporarily outside the porters' lodge and walked the short distance to the road to check for traffic. Having made sure the coast was clear, I ran back and pushed the trolley as hard as I could, so that by the time I reached the main road I was running and had built up considerable momentum. I raced the trolley across the road and set off up the hill on the opposite side at a fair speed. Things were going rather well and I was three-quarters of the way up when one of the front wheels suddenly snagged on a stone. The trolley jerked abruptly to a halt and veered to the right. It was now sideways on to the hill and with gravity beginning to exert its influence my load began inexorably to roll back. For a brief moment I was able to halt its downward progress by leaning hard against it, but ultimately the combined weight of trolley and corpse became too great for me. My feet began to slither and after a brief struggle I decided to jump aside deftly to avoid being run down.

It is quite true that, at moments like those, events do seem to occur in slow motion. I was glued to the spot, and all I could do was watch as the trolley slowly but relentlessly started to roll downhill towards the main road, accelerating rapidly all the while. It now became apparent to me that there was a still more pressing problem developing and this was that Waterworks Road itself was quite a steep hill leading down to Dereham Road about half a mile away. I desperately hoped therefore that the trolley would slow down and gradually come to a halt of its own volition, but sadly it didn't. The opposite happened. Once again it obeyed Newton's first law and executed a neat turn to the right, before setting off down the hill on the wrong side of the road and moving ever faster. I began to run after it but by the time it passed the Earl of Leicester public house near the bottom of the hill it was travelling at around twenty miles per hour. By now it was just after eleven p.m. and some late-night drinkers were leaving the pub. They seemed mildly surprised to observe an unattended hospital trolley speeding past in the direction of the city centre, followed a moment later by a lanky brown-coated figure racing after it, about thirty yards behind.

The junction of Waterworks Road and Dereham Road is a traffic-light controlled T-junction and, as luck would have it, the lights turned to green in the trolley's favour just as it approached the crossing. The speeding four-wheeled vehicle then careered across the junction and mounted the pavement on the opposite side, eventually coming to rest a few yards further down the road at the number 68 bus stop. Here it joined the tail of a small queue of people waiting, some of whom had just left the Earl of Leicester. As I approached, I could see one elderly man, cap in hand, scratching his head and staring in disbelief at the trolley, while the others looked on in some consternation.

When I arrived, breathless after my exertions, the old gentleman looked at me and, still scratching his head, asked, 'That trolley yours, son?'

'Yes, it's mine! Dreadfully sorry!' I panted.

'Where's it going?' I didn't like to say that I was on the way to the mortuary and that this had simply been an unexpected detour.

'It just rolled down the hill unexpectedly. Terribly sorry.' I made a move to grasp the handle at one end of the trolley. He was still scratching his head as he looked up and saw the number 68 approaching. My action was misconstrued.

'You'll never get it on the bus, son.'

'No! No! I'm from the West Norwich Hospital – I'm just taking it back.' The man had presumably spent the whole evening in the Earl of Leicester, as he doubtless did every Friday night, but he had never before been joined in the bus queue by a mortuary trolley and a long-haired hospital porter, and he was having some difficulty comprehending the significance of these events.

'Yes, good job, 'cos you'll never get it on the bus.' And with a final incredulous look, first at the trolley and then at me, he clambered on, still scratching his head.

After a final breathless apology to those still left at the bus stop, I set about pushing the trolley back as though nothing unusual had happened. Somehow I managed to negotiate Waterworks Road and then started to climb the hill leading to the hospital, before eventually reaching the mortuary. By this time I was exhausted and had to pause to catch my breath. As my panting diminished and my pulse settled I became acutely aware that it was now pitch-black and deafeningly silent. I began to feel distinctly edgy.

A dim bulb shone from a lantern above the mortuary door and in the half-light I unlocked the door and pushed the trolley inside. Growing more and more uneasy by the second, I opened the huge fridge doors and a chilling blast of cold air met me. Inside, I could see the stacked layers of corpses wrapped tightly in their ghostly white sheets. Gently I withdrew an unoccupied stretcher from the fridge and aligned my trolley alongside for the transfer. It was then, when the corpse was half-on and half-off the stretcher, that the deathly silence was suddenly shattered by a loud rattling noise. The fridge shook and shivered as though each cadaver was desperately trying to escape, and then, as the din subsided, the spine-chilling rattle was replaced by a low-pitched humming sound. At that, I lost all that remained of my self-control and panicked, rushing outside the building as fast as my legs could carry me, where, with my heart pumping like a piston, it slowly began to dawn on me that opening the fridge door had raised the temperature sufficiently for it to switch on automatically. Once I had regained some slight degree of composure, I gingerly edged my way back inside the mortuary and completed the transfer. With my well-travelled corpse safely inside, I slammed the fridge door shut and ran into the warm night air as fast as I could.

CHAPTER 6:

DOWN AND OUT IN CLAPHAM AND BRIXTON

After a summer largely spent working at the West Norwich Hospital, I returned to Liverpool Hall with a small sum of money in my bank account. It was the beginning of my second year and our lectures picked up seamlessly where they had left off before the summer break. This term we were dissecting the thorax, making frogs' legs twitch with weak electric currents and studying yet more obscure cycles in biochemistry.

'Hello, Spoz. Fancy coming to a party on Saturday?' It was my elder brother by five years, Peter – the Woog – who had phoned me. He was also living in London, working for an international law firm and staying in a friend's house at Clapham. His girlfriend happened to be a student nurse at St Thomas', and she shared a house with several other nurses on the opposite side of the Common.

'Of course. Thanks very much, Woog.'

'Haven't got a girlfriend, have you?'

'No. Not just at the moment – actually.'

'Good. Should be lots of spare apparently.'

'Really? Excellent!' My heart lifted. 'You're sure?'

'Bound to be. Should be in the bag.'

'Just the job,' I exclaimed. 'When and where?'

I spent most of that Saturday afternoon preparing for the event. First, I checked my condom status. Yes – all three were still there in my wallet, just as they had been for the past four years. Then I simply had to make myself irresistible to the opposite sex. Wearing a pair of tight, black, flared trousers, which contrasted with a virtually see-through white cotton shirt with a collar so long I could see the tips in my peripheral vision, and topped off by a deep red silk kerchief wound around my neck, I was in every respect a doppelgänger for Lord Byron. To complete the ensemble I wore my dark-blue Civil Defence WW2 greatcoat. Just in case I was sufficiently lucky to bring a girl back to my small study bedroom, I carefully made the bed, checked that I had some dry Martini left in the bottle on the windowsill, and switched my bedside light on. Satisfied that the ambience was as romantic as it ever could be, I then left to meet up with Arthur, William and Charles in the Lord Russell, a nearby pub.

When I arrived, the trio were already there, standing at the bar, deep in conversation. I walked over and joined them. 'Anyone want a drink?' I asked, taking my wallet out.

'See you've not used your condoms over the summer then, Grahame.' It was William. On this occasion I didn't take up the challenge.

'Look, d'you want a drink or not?'

'I'll have a pint of Pedigree, please,' he said slowly, with a smile.

'Same, please.' said the other two

Each with a fresh pint, we discussed our plans for the evening.

'I've been invited to a party in Clapham. Anybody want to come along?' I felt rather smug about this invitation.

'My father's come down to London and I'm meeting him for dinner,' said William, who had put on a shirt and tie in anticipation of a good meal in some smart restaurant.

'How about you two?' I said, looking at Arthur and Charles.

Arthur looked at his watch. 'I've still got that physiology essay to write.'

'But it's Saturday night. You're not going to work tonight, surely?' I had always put such homework off until the last possible moment.

'Yes, it's got to be in by Monday, you know. You done yours?'

'No. Of course not. But there's always tomorrow! That's what Sundays are for.' Arthur was not to be persuaded and Charles similarly was in no mood for a party, so at around eight o'clock I left by myself to take the tube to Clapham Common. Once there, I thought I should have another couple of pints in The Angel, a nice little hostelry I had visited before. Then I walked the half-mile or so to the Edwardian terraced street where the party was to be held.

By the time I arrived it was about ten o'clock and there was no need to check the house numbers to discover where the party was, since one door was wide open and loud music was emanating from within. I walked up the path and stepped through the front door where I encountered numerous couples in various stages of inebriation, standing in the hallway or seated on the stairs. I paused, and when a girl glanced toward me I asked her where the drinks were. She pointed upwards and so I gently nudged my way up the stairs past chatting and embracing couples. The bar proved to be in the kitchen, the floor of which was sticky with spilt beer, while on a table near the wall there was a jumble of bottles and cans. There, I helped myself to a beer. From the next room came loud music and, glass in hand, I proceeded to investigate. At the far end of the room – dark, and thick with cigarette smoke – I spotted my brother and his friends. The Woog, who also seemed to be dressed as Lord Byron, briefly acknowledged my wave, then carried on talking excitedly to his own coterie, clearly not wanting his younger brother to cramp his style.

Everyone seemed to know each another or at least to have a partner. I couldn't see an unaccompanied girl anywhere. 'So much for the spare,' I thought. I helped myself to another beer, lit a cigarette and stationed myself at the top of the stairs. In this strategic position, near the kitchen, the bathroom and the room where people were dancing, I could easily keep an eye on developments and reach the toilet when necessary. After an hour or so, trying to look cool at the top of the stairs, there was still no sign of any unaccompanied girls. I was beginning to think it might be sensible to accept that this had been yet another unsuccessful evening and that I should go home, when I saw a uniformed nurse gingerly ascending the stairs, carefully edging around people to avoid having drinks spilled on her dress. I watched her for a while and as she reached the landing she met my gaze and smiled.

'Didn't know it was a fancy dress party,' I said.

'No it's not,' she replied.

'I meant – haven't you come as a nurse? I'm Lord Byron for the night.'

'I've just finished a late shift.' She sighed, and then, in a decidedly plummy English accent, continued, 'I'm utterly worn out. I'm not sure I can be bothered to get changed. I really just want to go to bed, but I'll never get to sleep with all this racket going on.' I decided to drop my attempt at humour.

'Hi. I'm Grahame,'

'Oh.' She looked up with what seemed like a hint of interest. 'Rose,' she said, and shook my extended hand.

We talked in the relative quiet of the landing. She was five foot something, had a bright, intelligent face with an upturned nose and short dark hair cut in a bob. Nurses' uniforms are not designed to enhance a girl's figure (in fact the opposite is the case) but Rose looked both shapely and attractive. After a while she said, 'Well, I think 1 *will* go and get changed after all.' Then after a pause she added, 'Will you be staying?' I said I'd wait. She returned quite shortly, clad in a flowery, fresh summer dress, wearing a hint of make-up, and smelling deliciously of honeysuckle on a warm summer evening.

We spent all that night talking and dancing and the following day I woke up in Rose's bed, her warm naked body lying peacefully beside me.

* * *

At the end of the spring term we sat our first major set of exams. There was a great deal of factual information to be learned and hence a significant failure rate. From the start of that term I had put in a lot of work, essentially learning a wealth of texts by heart. This inevitably curtailed my social life, but I continued to see Rose on an intermittent basis. I was extremely pleased when I eventually surmounted those academic hurdles and was invited by Dr. Trimble to work towards a degree in Anatomy. Arthur and I now had to leave Commonwealth Hall and find accommodation elsewhere. On hearing that I was soon to be homeless, Dr Trimble's secretary told me that there was a vacancy in the house she shared with a rather eclectic group of friends. I was accordingly invited to view and be viewed and was duly accepted as the latest member of the household.

Compton Cottage was situated conveniently close to Clapham Common tube station, some shops, a number of pubs and of course, the house where Rose and her friends lived. The other residents of Compton Cottage, along with 'Weenie', my helpful medical secretary, included a girl called Elaine (a well-spoken personal assistant) and two men in their mid-twenties. Peter, the leaseholder, was a Naval Officer. He was extraordinarily good-looking, with long dark wavy hair, a neatly trimmed beard and bedroom eyes. He owned a green MG Midget and possessed a succession of very attractive girlfriends. The other male in the house was Bob, an overweight, beer-drinking computer programmer.

Socially, this was a stimulating mix and I was glad to move aside from the rugger-bugger type of culture of which I was beginning to tire. Bob worked in the City of London and at about five o'clock each afternoon would retire to a nearby pub with his colleagues, rarely arriving home sober. He would regularly fall asleep on the tube going home and miss his stop, only to be awakened by staff at Morden Station, which was at the end of the Northern Line. They knew him well and would put him back on a northbound train if they were still running. Evidence of fish and chips on the doorstep usually indicated that he had arrived home. Portions of his favourite evening meal would be deposited there as he wrestled to find his key and unlock the door, with any remaining food ending up in bed beside him. His diet of fish and chips, together with copious quantities of beer, was occasionally supplemented by home-cooking.

'Grahame,' he said to me one evening, 'How many eggs is it safe to eat?' As the medical student in residence, I was growing quite used to being asked health-related questions, usually about how much it was safe to drink or smoke, but this was a new one to me.

'What – all at one time?' I asked.

'Yes, I've just eaten a six-egg omelette and was wondering if it might kill me.'

'I don't really know, Bob,' I said, 'But my mother always said not to eat more than two a day or you got "egg-bound". I think she meant constipated.'

'Oh! That's all right then,' he replied, 'I've just brought four of them back up!'

I liked Bob. Apart from once trying to kill us all by setting fire to the settee when he fell asleep with a lighted cigarette, he was good value. His main problem was that when drunk – which was most evenings – he insisted on singing *I'm a weary and a lonesome traveller* at every opportunity. This was of course before the days of Karaoke but most pubs in London had live music with at the very least a piano and a small stage at one end of the lounge bar. After a few beers, Bob would wander up to the compère and offer to sing. If he hadn't been there before (if he had been he would not have been allowed entry) he would then be welcomed up on stage.

Bob couldn't play the guitar any more than he could sing and the whole performance was a parody or – perhaps more accurately – a farce. He would begin his act by loudly strumming the open strings of his guitar (throughout the whole of his performance he wouldn't make any attempt to play a chord) and he would then shout rather than sing, 'I'm a weary and a lonesome traveller.' This would then be repeated at a slightly higher pitch and even more loudly. After a third reprise, his shout would become a yell and he would close with, 'An' I'm a-travellin' on.' This would be followed by an expansive strum on the open strings. That constituted Bob's one and only verse and it would generally be repeated until he was forced off stage by the management. The problem for me came when he discovered that I could play the piano and wanted me to accompany him. His idea was that, while he strummed the open strings of his guitar, I would just lay my forearm across the keyboard to create a loud, crashing, atonal cacophony. As a matter of principle I refused to be any part of this.

It was in The Unicorn – a pub in Brixton – one Saturday night when the inevitable happened. This was an old-fashioned pub with an elderly working-class clientèle who liked a good sing-song. Bob, along with some friends and myself, had had a few beers and were enjoying the entertainment. Mid-way through the evening Bob announced, 'Right, I'm going to do my weary and lonesome traveller,' and promptly rose to his feet. That was normally the cue for the rest of us to leave, in order to avoid being thrown out later, but for some reason on this occasion we were slow to act, something which I later came to regret. There was a piano on the small stage and on seeing this, Bob said, 'C'mon, Grahame, we can do our duet – you know – as we discussed, you play the piano and I'll do the guitar and sing.'

'No! Bob. No *way* am I going up there,' I said firmly.

'All right then,' he said defiantly, 'I'll do it myself,' and he set off unsteadily in the direction of the stage. The compère, who obviously didn't recognise him, welcomed him up on stage and handed him the microphone. Bob was in his element. 'Thank you very much, ladies and gen'lemen,' he said with an appalling mid-Atlantic accent, 'My name's Barb an I'm a-gonna sing for you *I'm a weary and lonesome traveller*.' There was an enthusiastic round of applause and some whistling. He then added, 'And now, ladies an' gen'lemen, I'd like a big round of applause for Grahame, my pianist.' Then, with an expansive gesture toward the table at which I was sitting, he added, 'Come on up, Grahame.'

As he spoke, my heart sank; I knew this could only end badly. I remained in my seat as the cheering and the whistling got louder. 'Grahame's a bit shy. Applause, ladies an' gen'lemen! Please welcome *Grahame Howard.*' The crowd grew louder and started to chant '*Grahame – Grahame*'. The others at my table encouraged me to get up and join Bob, mainly to divert attention from themselves, but I remained seated for about a further ten seconds, before I gave in to the inevitable. As I stood up the crowd cheered, and it was with a sense of impending doom that I walked slowly to the stage and seated myself at the piano.

'Thank you, ladies and gen'lemen,' said Bob and then, when the noise settled down, he announced in a lower tone as he cradled his guitar, 'Weary and lonesome traveller, here we go. A – one – two.' I was now in a difficult position. If I struck the keyboard with my forearm as Bob's atonal performance dictated, I would immediately be thrown out of the pub and probably banned for good. I did the only thing I could; as Bob strummed his opening chord and shouted, 'I'm a weary and a lonesome traveller,' I began to play one of the few pieces of music I knew by heart – the theme from the *Warsaw Concerto*. This is an impressive piece, with lots of arpeggios which make a pianist sound and look good.

Bob turned angrily to me between lines. 'What on earth are you playing? Use your elbow! *Use your elbow,*' he hissed. I continued to play the concerto and after two verses from Bob the crowd started booing and we were escorted off stage. I thought the overall effect had been musically rather interesting but Bob was distraught. 'That was *rubbish*. What on earth did you play that *rubbish* for? You ruined it.' Then, demonstrating a complete lack of insight into this débacle, he ended by announcing, 'We'll never be able to perform here again!'

After this tirade we walked back to our group of friends and as we passed one table, an old lady looked up at me and said, 'Oh, that was lovely, dear. That's the theme from *Dangerous Moonlight,* isn't it? Wasn't that David Niven a lovely man? Shame about your friend.'

The money I had accumulated from my summer job had now long been spent and once more I was impecunious. I was the recipient of a grant which paid my university fees, but it was means-tested and I relied on this being topped up by my father, the Dod, whose additional funding was unpredictable at best – and became non-existent after he was declared bankrupt. I had the smallest and therefore the cheapest room in Compton Cottage but that was still more than I could afford and early in the New Year I had run out of money completely. Luckily, I had one of my brighter income-generating ideas. I would live in the garage and sub-let my room.

As leaseholder, Peter was not entirely happy with this idea but eventually agreed. The plan was that I should spend the day at lectures, use the facilities of the house in the evening and then sleep in the garage. The garage was not currently being used to house a car and was an integral part of the house, brick-built and accessible from the hallway via an internal door. The only problem was that there was no heating in the garage. Moreover there happened to be a bitterly cold spell, with hard frost on the ground when I came to vacate my small cosy bedroom.

It was late in the evening when I first entered my new sleeping accommodation. I undressed in the relative warmth of the hallway, but a gust of freezing air greeted me as soon as I opened the door to the garage and stepped inside. I unzipped my cheap Woolworth's sleeping bag, crawled inside and set my alarm clock. It was perishing. I lay on the concrete floor and shivered. Luckily, I had my WW2 Civil Defence greatcoat, which I'd bought from the Army and Navy Surplus Stores in Norwich some years before. I spread the coat over my sleeping bag and tried to get to sleep. The coat staved off hypothermia, but it was still bitterly cold and the concrete floor was rock-hard.

Next morning, after very little sleep, I peeped out of the door, and finding everyone else had gone to work, came back into the warmth of the house and dressed for lectures.

That evening Peter asked, 'Did you get much sleep?'

'No,' I replied. 'It's freezing in there.'

'I'm not sure this is a good idea,' he continued. I agreed, but my room was gone for a month and there was no alternative. I was also stubborn and determined to show that my money-saving idea would work.

That night I put a blanket under my sleeping bag, but the concrete floor was no warmer or softer as a result and again I slept only fitfully. The weather was against me. It grew no warmer and, after seven long sleepless nights in the garage, I finally accepted that this could not go on. My studies were suffering and somnolence in lectures was becoming a real problem – I needed warmth *and* money

On occasion I would go to the Tate Gallery with Simon, a student in my year who maintained a deep interest in the visual arts. The Tate was conveniently close to St Thomas', being just across the Thames, and we had an agreement – he taught me about art and I took him to concerts, usually on the South Bank, and educated him as much as I could about music. A visit to the Tate seemed particularly attractive at this time, as entrance was free to students, it was warm inside and the coffee was cheap. On the Saturday of my first week sleeping in the garage, Simon and I agreed to go to the Pre-Raphaelite exhibition and it was over a coffee afterwards that I shared with him my accommodation problem. He was amazed.

'You're sleeping in a *garage*?' he said.

I became slightly defensive. 'Yes. Strictly speaking, it's a garage, but there's no car in it – obviously.' I then added, 'Though on reflection if there was, it would be a damn sight warmer.'

'Look, you could sleep on the floor at my place in Brixton for a short while if that would help. Have you thought,' he went on, 'of working on the building site next to the hospital? I did over the summer and labouring pays well.'

I gratefully took up his offer of a space on his sitting room floor, and the following week started the first of several lengthy stints as a labourer. This was on the building site adjacent to St Thomas' Hospital that was destined to become the new ward block. After a day's labouring I would head back to Brixton and copy out Simon's lecture notes for the day, waiting until everyone had gone to bed so that I could claim my share of floor-space, climb into my sleeping bag and try to get some sleep. After three weeks, my sub-let being over, I had earned enough money to pay the rent for a little while longer, and it was with great relief therefore that I moved back into my small but warm room in Compton Cottage.

That evening I decided to celebrate with a few pints at the Windmill, a pub on Clapham Common. It was still bitterly cold and snow lay on the ground as all of us from Compton Cottage walked the short distance across the Common to the pub, where we met up with Simon and a few of his friends from nearby Brixton. As usual after a couple of pints, Bob wanted to perform *I'm a weary and lonesome traveller*, and worryingly, there was a baby grand piano in the large lounge bar.

'No, Bob. I'm not doing it. You know what happened last time.'

'But that's because you didn't play it properly. If you'd done what I said, rather than play that fancy rubbish, we wouldn't have been banned.'

'Look, Bob, there are only so many pubs in Clapham and we can't afford to be banned from any more!'

'Okay,' he said. 'If you won't let me sing, let's get some girls down here!'

'We *do* have girls,' Peter explained, gesturing towards Weenie and Elaine. They, however, were with their boy friends.

'No! *Real* girls! – *Nurses*. Grahame, get those nurses you know down here.' He was getting pretty drunk by now and was referring to Rose and her flatmates whom he had met on a few occasions.

'I'm not phoning them,' I said. 'They're busy and it's nearly closing time.'

'Okay. *I* will! Give me their number.'

I refused initially but eventually gave in under pressure and reluctantly wrote Rose's phone number on a piece of paper. Bob went to the payphone and dialled the number with some difficulty. We couldn't hear the conversation but it was not long before he returned disconsolately to the table and sat down.

'What did she say, Bob?' I asked.

'Well, that's what's strange. I didn't say who I was, but as soon as Rose answered and said, "Hello", I just asked if anyone wanted six inches of steaming flesh rammed up between their thighs.'

'That's quite a direct approach,' I said. 'What did she say?'

'She just said, "Oh. Hi, Bob. Having a good time, are you? No, we're busy this evening. Give my love to Grahame, will you?" and hung up.'

CHAPTER 7:

SHORT WHITE COATS

Financial and accommodation problems aside, my year studying anatomy had been most agreeable. The teaching programme was light and much of the work could be done from home – that is, when I had one. Compton Cottage had an extensive selection of paperbacks and amongst these I discovered Alexander Solzhenitsyn, Scott Fitzgerald, Robert Graves – and also Somerset Maugham, who had walked the wards of St Thomas' as a medical student before becoming a man of letters. The garage incident and time spent labouring had undoubtedly affected my performance adversely but I was able to scrape a decent degree, and start my training as a clinical student the following autumn. This additional year of study meant that I had lost touch with my dissecting partners: Joan, Eddie, Pete and Mike; but Arthur, St John, Charles, Simon and William had also taken a year out and thus we started our clinical training together.

At one o'clock precisely, on the first day of the new term, I pushed open the glass doors of the building adjacent to St Thomas' House and entered the laundry store. There, standing behind the waist-high counter, was Ron whom I'd met on my very first day as a student. Boxer, barman and (between one and two o'clock each weekday) distributor of white coats, he had not changed noticeably in those three years, and the same tortoiseshell spectacles were perched at an oblique angle across his rubbery face.

'Congratulations, squire! Clinical now, are we?'

'Yes, Ron. May I therefore have one of your very best *short* white coats, please.' I emphasised the word 'short', as this style of coat signalled that I had passed my pre-clinical exams and was now well on the way to becoming a doctor. *Long* white coats were the preserve of those who were fully qualified.

'You've lost a bit of weight, squire. A forty – and long, I should think.' Then from under the counter he produced a neatly folded white linen jacket, which I immediately donned.

'Yes. That'll be you, squire.' Ron's jowls wobbled, the nearest he ever got to a smile.

'Perfect! Thanks, Ron. See you later in the bar.' So saying, and wearing my new badge of honour, I proudly stepped back through the doors and headed for St Thomas' House.

In addition to our short white coats we could now sport a stethoscope, usually placed discretely in the right hip pocket. This was, and indeed still is, the imprimatur of being a doctor. The trick was to have just sufficient tubing protruding in order to establish your status, without appearing pretentious. I hadn't as yet obtained a stethoscope, having discovered with amazement how expensive they were, and had a sense of déjà-vu from three years before when I realised that I couldn't afford a skeleton or even half the books I was expected to buy.

Back in St Thomas' House, I entered the canteen and spotted Arthur sitting reading a newspaper, a half-drunk cup of coffee on the table in front of him. As clinical students, we would be seeing – and indeed examining – patients, so there was now a strict dress code to be followed. Arthur's appearance hadn't changed greatly since we first met; but his straw-coloured hair was now freshly cut and neatly combed, while underneath his short white coat he wore a badly-pressed blue shirt and was sporting a tie for the first time in three years. In addition, he had what appeared to be a large snake wrapped around his neck.

'Nice stethoscope,' I said. 'Expensive?'

'Yes. A bit costly but these *are* the best for hearing those soft diastolic murmurs,' he announced as I sat down. I wasn't entirely sure what a diastolic murmur was, soft or otherwise, but I had a feeling that I was about to find out.

'For diastolic murmurs you use this bell-shaped thing, and for listening to the lungs you turn this knob here and use the diaphragm.' He then proceeded to twiddle the knobs on the end of his stethoscope while pretending to listen to his coffee cup.

'Wow! That's immense,' I said, but my sarcasm went unnoticed. I had been able to get through my pre-clinical years without a skeleton and initially tried to manage my clinical studies without a stethoscope. A few weeks later, however, I successfully bought a second-hand one quite cheaply from a student in the year above.

In the seventies, clinical teaching was largely delivered on an apprenticeship model. There were certainly some formal lectures and tutorials, but a large proportion of our time was spent on the wards. The routine involved taking a history of the patient's symptoms and then carrying out a clinical examination. We would also attend operations as well as learning practical skills such as taking blood and performing electrocardiographs. It was the era of, 'See one, do one, teach one'.

For teaching purposes, five or six students were allocated to a 'firm'. Each comprised a consultant or two, senior and junior registrars, sometimes a senior house officer and the finally those most junior of doctors, the housemen. Over the course of our clinical training we would form the members of two surgical and two medical firms, while also spending time with specialist teams in such fields as obstetrics, gynaecology and paediatrics. There were few, if any, attendance records kept and no designated university holidays, so we tended to take time off during less intensive periods of teaching.

For my first surgical firm I was allocated to the professorial unit. The two professors were both extremely eminent in their respective fields. Professor McIntyre was the senior and had

89

written the standard text on diseases of the lymphatic system. During his operating sessions he always insisted upon employing – from amongst the students – one 'dirty' and one 'clean' dresser. To this day I don't fully understand what all this meant, but I suspect it dated back to the days of Lord Lister in Edinburgh and the early use of antiseptics.

On my first appearance in the operating theatre I was allocated the dubious honour of being the 'clean' dresser. This duty came with no perks and put me centre-stage – or in this case centre-theatre – a position I did *not* relish. In this role, I was required to scrub up and, as a member of the operating team, one of my tasks was to cut the professorial stitches. It was particularly unfortunate that this event took place at a time when the left lens of my spectacles was loose and kept falling out. While I could replace it easily enough, it would spontaneously drop out at the most inopportune of moments. Without the lens I could see perfectly well with my right eye but there was only a blur in my left and stereoscopic vision was thus completely lost.

Under normal circumstances the unpredictable behaviour of my left lens was not a problem but I envisaged that it might be so in my new role as 'clean' dresser. Accordingly, before scrubbing up, I had taken the precaution of deliberately removing the offending lens from its frame to ensure that it didn't fall out during the operation – a wise precaution, or so I thought. The problem was, however, that the consequent lack of stereoscopic vision made stitch cutting very difficult indeed. As the operation was drawing to its close, the professor held up his first stitch and said, 'Cut, please.' I had waited nearly two hours for this crucial moment and immediately advanced my scissors (supplied specially for the purpose), and snipped. I missed the stitch completely, my scissors being about two inches away to the left. It was similar to that occasion the previous year when I had kept missing the rugby ball when trying to kick it into touch.

'*Cut, please.*' The professor repeated, more loudly this time.

I tried for a second time. I was closer, but not close enough and so missed again. Now the whole surgical team – nurses, junior surgeons and the professor – were looking at me in amazement. I began to sweat and my hands shook, but at the third attempt I succeeded.

'Is there a problem?' the professor asked quietly while continuing to stitch.

'I'm afraid my glasses are broken, sir.' I mumbled. 'I've only got one lens.' This explanation wasn't helping. The professor slowly lifted his head and scrutinised me. He uttered no words, but his expression said it all; and it was unrepeatable. I was forthwith relieved of my duties, pending repair of my spectacles – an eminently wise decision as there were at least a hundred more stitches to cut and we all wanted to get home that day.

For the remaining operating sessions I resumed my customary position at the back of the throng where, being tall, I was able to see what was going on without being too close to the action. I thought I had regained some credibility with the aforementioned professor when I saved his daughter's life. Well, if not her life, I certainly saved her from severe bruising and probable concussion. As usual when the professor was operating, there was a mêlée of junior staff and students gathered around the table. On this occasion, I was behind one young lady who was standing on a small platform sometimes used by surgeons to obtain a better view of the proceedings. I didn't see her coming, but suddenly she was cradled in my arms. She had fainted, fallen backwards and without thinking I had put my arms out and caught her. With the help of some other students who had seen her fall, I laid her gently on the floor, where she rapidly came round. Several people quietly congratulated me and I subsequently learned that she was the professor's daughter. Sadly, my valiant deed went unrecognised as the professor continued to operate, totally oblivious to my heroism.

'Brilliant catch, Grahame. Absolutely brilliant, just effortless.' William congratulated me over a beer in the bar afterwards. 'Imagine saving the life of the professor's daughter!'

'Oh! Anyone would have done the same.' I said modestly while taking a sip of my beer.

'That should guarantee you a house job on the professorial team.' But sadly William was to be proved wrong.

Along with attendance at operations, ward rounds were the mainstay of our clinical teaching. We would each be allocated a patient, take a history of the patient's illness and examine him or her before presenting the case to the professor and the rest of the students. On professorial ward rounds there might often be as many as fifteen individuals clustered around the patient's bed at any one time and it could be difficult for the more enthusiastic students to get sufficiently close to the patient.

Most of us were content to hover at the back, but in any group there is always one slightly nerdy student who simply has to be the centre of attention, by standing at the bedside and answering all the questions. Gerald was one such person, and his behaviour was beginning to irritate all of us. He was short, at about five and a half feet, slim, and under his white coat always wore one of those sleeveless, coarsely knitted, woollen pullovers – the type which any self-respecting boy had abandoned when he left primary school. He had black curly hair and wore tortoiseshell spectacles with lenses as thick as the base of a milk bottle.

It was the occasion of the professorial ward round and Professor McIntyre, tall and athletic, was striding out, setting a fast pace. He was at the head of our group of fifteen or so staff and students who were strung out behind him in the long, wide, cathedral-like corridor linking the main wards in the original Victorian section of the hospital. As always, Gerald was at the head of the pack and virtually jogging to keep up. In his left hand he clutched a sheaf of notes relating to the patient we were about to see and he was forced to slow to a walking pace in order to read these one last time. In so doing, he lost his pole position as the rest of us overtook him. Realising this, Gerald stuffed the notes in his pocket and started to push his way forward to be first at the bedside. As he attempted to squeeze his way past William and myself, we simultaneously decided to block his path. Realising that we wouldn't let him through, he dropped back in order to attempt the same manoeuvre on the opposite side of the corridor. We countered and held him back physically until we had reached the bedside, where all of us formed an impenetrable barrier around the patient, with Gerald trapped behind.

Poor Gerald was now desperate. He scampered around the back of our group from one side to the other, desperately trying to find a gap in this human barrier and so reach the bedside, but every time he tried to push through we closed ranks. He then began to jump up and down in a vain attempt to see over our heads, but this could do no more than offer momentary glimpses of the patient. Eventually he gave up and wandered around at the back of the group, reading his notes and mumbling to himself. The patient in question had a lump in his abdomen and, one at a time, the rest of us dutifully examined this object of clinical interest while the others kept Gerald well away from the bedside. When everyone had finished, and we were discussing the diagnosis, William and I were amazed to see Gerald's small hand appear from between a girl's legs, as tentatively he reached out toward the patient in order to palpate the still exposed abdomen.

Unlike Gerald, I always endeavoured to hover at the back so as to avoid being asked any questions. Occasionally I would not be quick enough with my positioning and would end at the front of the group and hence become the centre of attention. The next patient to be examined on this particular ward round was a young woman with Crohn's disease and as a result of all the jostling for position in order to keep Gerald at the back, I found myself next to the patient, completely trapped at her bedside. Arthur, stethoscope around his neck, was presenting the clinical history and demonstrating how one should listen for bowel sounds. The patient herself had intermittent bowel obstruction and was hoping that her bowels would resume working spontaneously and thus avoid an operation. We took it in turns to listen to her abdomen using our new stethoscopes and then there followed some discussion about the different types of bowel sound and their significance. This patient had very few – a distinctly bad sign.

What happened next was unfortunate and probably occurred because I hadn't eaten for some time. At that time, during periods of severe financial restraint, several days might pass without my having a meal. It was just as we were ending our discussion on bowel sounds that my own abdomen gave vent to the most tremendous rumble, a borborygmic extravaganza. The sound resembled the flushing of one of those old-fashioned cisterns, where the tank is located on the wall high above the toilet, and upon pulling the chain the water is released to tumble in a torrent down to the bowl below. This initial flushing noise is then followed by the prolonged tinkling sound of the tank slowly refilling. My truly seismic gurgle lasted at least ten seconds and could be heard clearly by all those gathered around the bed. Those standing beside me started to giggle and I was just about to apologise profusely, when the professor turned toward the patient – who was now gazing down at her own abdomen with a puzzled expression – looked her directly in the eyes, and pronounced, 'That's a very good sign. Well done! Excellent!'

Following three months on the surgical firm we rotated and I found myself with Simon and some others on my first medical firm, which was based at the nearby Lambeth Hospital. The teaching rounds there were similar but tended to involve more talking and less activity than the surgical equivalent. Like me, Simon preferred to linger at the rear of the student group, allowing the most eager ones (like Gerald) to be close to the patient and to answer the questions. It was in consequence of this that I happened to be the first to spot the dead man. While our teacher, a consultant physician, was expounding on the various types of chest disease that might afflict the good folk of Lambeth, my mind began to wander and I happened to glance toward the neighbouring bed on which lay an elderly man. Something, I felt, wasn't quite right and so I looked a bit more carefully. He was lying extremely still and didn't appear to be breathing. I nudged Simon and whispered, 'I think that chap's dead!'

Simon initially thought I was joking but did glance across and after a moment replied in a whisper, 'Yes, I think you're right.' There were visitors on the ward and it didn't seem entirely appropriate to yell, '*I think there's a dead man here.*' So we made efforts to attract the attention of our teacher, who was now talking about the causes of chronic bronchitis and was asking what we thought might be the diagnosis of the patient whose bed we surrounded.

'*Excuse me! Excuse me!*' I called loudly, waving my arms wildly.

The consultant obviously misconstrued this excited behaviour as enthusiasm to answer his question.

'Yes, Howard? What would be on your differential diagnosis here?' he asked with a smile.

'I think he's dead, sir!' I half-mouthed and half-whispered these words while pointing to the next bed. Those close enough to hear turned to look at me with undisguised surprise.

'I couldn't hear you. Do please speak up, Howard,' replied the consultant, a degree of impatience creeping into his voice.

'I think he's dead, sir.' This time I said it loudly enough for all to hear.

On hearing this the patient expressed considerable concern, while the consultant, initially bemused, became irritated. This was certainly not in line with his own differential diagnosis and he began to tick me off.

'What do you mean? You think he's dead? He's talking to us, isn't he? So he can't possibly be dead. Don't be such an ass, Howard.'

'I think he's possibly dead, sir. I mean the man in the bed next to him.' Once again I tried to indicate the individual I was alluding to without letting everyone on the ward – staff and visitors alike – know that there was a dead body lying in one of the beds unbeknown to anyone else.

The consultant was now growing increasingly annoyed, but nevertheless did glance towards where I was pointing. On seeing the motionless figure lying in the next bed, he brusquely pushed through the crowd and noisily drew the curtains around the lifeless patient.

As we drifted out of the ward, Simon said quietly, 'Good diagnosis, Grahame. Shame you're not so astute with living patients.'

Thus it came about that our diagnostic and therapeutic skills were gradually honed to perfection. We all made errors of course; it was just that some made more than others. Bill's suggestions that being a spaceman was the commonest cause of osteoporosis, or that it was quite normal to find gonococci in the throat of perfectly healthy people, are just two instances of the more memorable errors that I can recall. Bill himself was excellent company; short and muscular, he was pleasant looking, even though he still had the stigmata of facial acne. He spent most of his spare time pursuing his two main interests: drinking and sex, and it was possibly as a result of the lapse of concentration as his mind wandered, to the latter in particular, that he seemed especially disposed to the odd gaffe. During the introductory tutorial for the obstetrics and gynaecology course, when we were asked if any of us had previously carried out a vaginal examination, it was Bill, who, in all seriousness, answered, 'Only socially, sir!'

CHAPTER 8:

PUBAR

Later that year I found myself homeless once again, only this time not for financial reasons. After living in Compton Cottage contentedly for over a year, Peter our landlord chose to work abroad and I was consequently forced to find somewhere else to live. Arthur and William invited me to join them and two other students from our year to share a house they had rented in Battersea, an offer I accepted with alacrity. This grey, Victorian, mid-terrace house was situated on Queenstown Road, just south of Chelsea Bridge. It had four floors – that is, if you included the separate basement flat where an old couple lived. The best rooms had by now all been claimed and I was accordingly allocated the one remaining, which was at the rear of the top floor. From there, unbeknown to me when I accepted the offer, the occupant could clearly hear the Tannoy announcements from Battersea Park Station without having to get out of bed, while at night the room was brightly illuminated by the station floodlights. We called the house PUBAR. This was derived from FUBAR, the name of a rally car team for which one of my school friends had driven. PUBAR stood for 'pissed up beyond all recognition', and William decided to paint the name vertically in huge white letters on the black front door. Running down the left-hand side of the door one read PUBAR, while on the right-hand side HOUSE was painted. Subsequently, we regularly received mail addressed to Pubar House, Battersea, and on one occasion when Arthur was on a bus passing our new home he heard a child ask his mother, 'Is that where Pooh Bear lives, Mummy?'

Within fifteen minutes of moving in, Arthur had set up his room, just as he had in Topsham Road years before. The same tapestry and posters were on the wall, while his wooden box from school, neatly packed with everything he considered of importance, was placed in front of the empty fireplace. His allocated space was the rear section of a large ground-floor room stretching from the front to the rear of the house and divided in two by closed wooden internal doors. The front room was occupied by St John Smiler – or that was how he was known. St John was of average height, broad-shouldered and muscularly built – as befitted a first team rugby player – and his short light-brown hair was parted low down on the left side of his head just an inch above his ear. He dressed in the same way all year round, no matter what the season or weather. A creased white shirt was invariably accompanied by a tie and baggy corduroy trousers. He never wore socks (I'm not sure if he owned any) and on his bare feet he wore leather sandals all the year round. St John made no attempt whatsoever to be fashionable and, of us all, he was the one who had the weakest grip on sanity. He had many eclectic interests, including poetry – which he wrote – and music, being able to play both the cello and piano. His accomplishments also extended to sport, being a talented swimmer and rugby player. Sadly he had no sense of propriety and would practise his cello whenever the mood took him, which was often in the early hours of the morning.

Arthur now had a girlfriend, a student nurse called Jess, who on occasion would spend the night at PUBAR. If St John knew she was staying, he would wait until they had both retired to bed, then settle his cello between his legs and start to serenade Jess with what he thought was romantic music. Unfortunately, he was very much out of practice and his preferred music, which included Schubert's *Marche Militaire* and the *Sabre Dance* by Khachaturian, was less than erotic. His performance was thus not quite the melodious romantic music he intended and the disjointed series of screeches and squeaks, accompanied by frequent expletives from himself, did not in any way facilitate Arthur's nocturnal advances. After a few nights of this, Arthur could take no more and so, during one of these musical interludes – pausing only to put on his underpants – he stormed next door. In the middle of the room he found St John in his dressing gown, his cello between his legs, peering intently at some music on the stand in front of him.

'For God's sake, St John, *please* shut up. I'm trying to get some sleep.' St John looked up from his music and then, after a final unsuccessful attempt to produce the desired note, lifted his bow from the strings.

'Oh, I thought you had Jess with you and that a little romantic music might help get her in the mood.'

'That's not a little mood music. It's awful. It's a squeaky catophany.' He had meant to say a screechy cacophony but in his irate state was becoming dysphasic. St John seemed genuinely upset.

'Oh! Yes. Sorry about the high B flat. That *was* a bit off, I know.' He stroked the bow over the top string to demonstrate how it should have sounded. Arthur was growing more and more exasperated

'No, it's not the bloody B flat, it's the whole bloody thing. It's *awful*! I'm trying to get to sleep and I don't need your *bloody* mood music.' So saying, Arthur slammed the door and went back to his own bedroom. St John was puzzled and felt genuinely hurt, since he'd truly believed he had been doing Arthur a favour, but to Jess and Arthur's great relief he ceased his romantic interludes thereafter.

It was St John who decided that a house containing six young, male, testosterone-filled, medical students should have a birth control policy. In this respect he was well ahead of his time. He went to the local surgery and put his case to one of the GP's. Amazingly, he came away with a prescription for a gross of condoms to be shared amongst us. Having done all the work (as he saw it) he then decided that he should be their custodian – a kind of condom comptroller – and so he stored them safely in a cupboard by his bed, on the wall above which was displayed a large chart documenting their usage. If we thought our luck was in, we were expected to go and ask him for one – or two, if we felt really lucky – and he would duly dispense them and update his chart. There was a potential problem, however, in that St John's motorbike – a BSA Bantam 125 – had broken down. Most of us would have taken it to a garage but St John decided to dismantle it down to its smallest components, which he then laid out carefully on the floor of his bedroom. Since being banned from playing his cello, he now amused himself by tinkering with the cycle parts late into the night in a vain attempt to reassemble them in the right order.

The first time that William brought Jane back to PUBAR, he realised that he was likely to need the services of the condom comptroller. William's bedroom was on the top floor and so, with a brief remark to Jane, 'I won't be long – just got to nip downstairs for something,' he put on his underpants and rushed down the three flights of stairs to St John's room. With a brief knock at the door he burst in and made directly for the cabinet where he knew the supply was kept. Half-way across the room, however, he stubbed his toe against the motorbike's cylinder head. With an agonised yell of pain he rapidly withdrew his foot only to stand on a spark plug and various other sharp engine components. Wincing, he then raised his right leg, which destabilised him completely, and fell backwards into the frame of what had once been a Bantam 125. This had been propped against a bookcase which subsequently began to topple and, with an almighty crash, William, bits of bike and bookcase all fell together in a tangled confusion on the floor of the bedroom.

'Hey! Mind my bike,' said St John, who had been wakened by the noise.

'You *bastard*! You complete and utter *bastard*!' William was holding his foot.

'Mind the bike,' St John cautioned. 'The parts are all in a certain order.' William was not concerned about the order of the bike bits – all he wanted was a condom.

'You *bastard*! Give me a condom,' he demanded.

'You could at least say "please",' responded St John as he duly handed over the requisite object of William's visit.

Eventually, condom in hand, William raced upstairs again. The noise had been considerable and he was now bleeding from numerous superficial wounds with copious amounts of engine oil smeared across his face. Back upstairs, Jane was sound asleep and snoring quietly. The moment was lost.

My personal contribution to the house was the addition of a piano. I had bought this from the local Oxfam shop and, for the magnificent sum of twelve pounds, became the proud owner of a fine-looking, late-Victorian upright piano of inlaid mahogany with two folding brass candlesticks on the front. A volunteer from the shop brought it round in a van and together we pulled and dragged it up the two flights of stairs to my bedroom. As the piano ascended, small pieces of felt began to fall from it on to the stairs. These were the dampers, an essential component of this sophisticated instrument, without which a piano sounds as if it is being played in an echo chamber. After the piano had been safely stowed in my room, I retrieved all the scraps of felt and, with the help of some Evostick, glued them back to the mechanism as best I could. Interestingly, this didn't make a significant difference to the timbre of the instrument, which continued to sound like a honky-tonk in some wild-west saloon, whatever style of music I played.

That night I decided to celebrate the arrival of my new acquisition with an impromptu inaugural recital. Rose came round with several of her friends and, against the background of some particularly interesting Tannoy announcements from Battersea Park Station, I played a little Chopin, *The Entertainer* by Scott

Joplin and then, to finish with a flourish, my own version of the theme from the *Warsaw Concerto*. The lack of a complete set of dampers in the instrument meant that all the pieces sounded somewhat similar and much akin to *Roll Out The Barrel* but my guests were polite enough to applaud and after the performance we all adjourned to the nearby Mason's Arms for a few drinks. Rose decided to stay the night and after the others had gone their various ways, we gratefully retired to bed.

St. John – with his motorbike now fixed – had travelled to Brixton to spend the evening wooing a nurse with the aid of some homespun sonnets and serenades. At about three in the morning I heard the front door bang. Heavy footsteps followed, stamping up the stairs, and then suddenly my bedroom door burst open. I sat up bolt upright as Rose pulled the sheets over her head.

'What the hell are you doing? Who are you?' I shouted. In the semi-darkness I could just make out the form of a man, clad in a knee length leather jacket and wearing a motorcycle helmet, with goggles still covering his eyes. On his hands were thick leather gauntlets. Without a word he walked directly to the piano, sat down at the keyboard and – gauntlets still on – began to play *The Maple Leaf Rag*. I soon realised who it was.

'St John! You complete *arse*.' I yelled furiously. 'D'you realise what time it is?' And then, answering my own question: 'It's the middle of the bloody night, *that's* what time it is. For God's sake stop making that racket.'

He continued to play a few more bars then halted. 'Heard you'd got a piano. Great idea. Thought I'd just try it out.' And with that, he began to play again. The *Maple Leaf Rag* requires both manual dexterity and a delicacy of touch which is difficult at the best of times, and completely impossible while wearing motorcycle gauntlets. I started to get out of bed but suddenly realising I was stark naked, thought better of it and merely commanded, 'St. John! Get out of my room. *Now*!'

Eventually he stopped playing. 'Doesn't sound too good! Must be out of tune.' Then he peered through his goggles at his hands and seemed decidedly surprised to discover that he was still wearing his gauntlets. 'Of course the goggles and the gloves don't help.' Thereupon, he noisily closed the keyboard lid and made to stand up.

'For God's sake, St John, do please bugger off and leave us alone.' I was becoming increasingly annoyed. Rose then popped her head above the sheet to see what was going on.

'Oh. Hello, Rose. Didn't see you there. Nice piano, Grahame. We'll be able to perform duets now. Tell you what, I'll just nip downstairs and get my cello and the piano part to the *Sabre Dance*. It's not too difficult and we can entertain Rose with a short performance. No time like the present.' St John started to take his gauntlets and helmet off in preparation.

'*No!*' Rose and I shouted in unison. At this, St John finally stood up and banged downstairs without a further word. I locked the door and clambered back into bed.

* * *

PUBAR had mice. They lived in the old coal-cellar which was accessed from the kitchen. We were not unduly bothered by this, not least because we spent little time there, yet our visiting girlfriends seemed to find it a trifle unsettling to have mice running playfully about their feet when they were trying to cook something especially delicious. It was St John who saw a placard in the window of the nearby Masons' Arms, announcing: 'Free Kittens to a Good Home', and decided that this was the solution to our murine problem. All at once he seemed to be highly knowledgeable on the subject of cats. He informed us that these felines weren't natural mousers but required to be taught. Accordingly he drew up an intensive training programme to convert our timid new kitten into a top-class mouse exterminator. Central to the learning process was the possession of a dead mouse to practise upon, and St John was able to secure one from an undisclosed source.

That evening therefore, we all gathered in the kitchen to observe the inaugural training session. To begin with, St John tied a length of string to the dead mouse's tail. He then suspended the corpse over the coal-cellar stairs where the live mice had made their home. 'It's crucially important that the cat shouldn't actually *catch* the mouse,' he informed us 'It should just chase it and not eat it. Eating a mouse may make a cat ill. It's quite like fox-hunting.' This analogy was, I think, totally lost on the rest of us.

'Do we all have to saddle up and ride around blowing horns?' I asked.

'What's the point,' interposed William, 'if the cat doesn't catch the mice? Do they just surrender?' Obviously he was not at all convinced either. Arthur was more direct.

'St John. You're talking absolute rubbish.'

St. John ignored all of those comments in order to concentrate on the finer points of his training schedule. After a lengthy period of inactivity (which he attributed to the kitten having mistakenly been fed twice at lunchtime) and with much encouragement from all the bystanders, our trainee hunter began to chase the dangling mouse. St John became quite ecstatic when the kitten reared up on its hind legs and waved its little front paws at the flying bait. He then initiated phase two of the training programme – which was to lure the kitten to where the live mice were. With a flamboyant gesture, he tossed the dead mouse, still attached to its string, down the cellar stairs. The kitten dashed after it, and after a second or two St John – rather like an angler reeling in a salmon – attempted to retrieve the mouse. It would not move. 'Must have got stuck on something,' he observed and, undeterred, pulled the string harder.

'For God's sake, it's bad enough having live mice down there, never mind adding some dead ones. Are you quite sure you know what you're doing?' This came from William, who was clearly not impressed with the training programme so far. A moment later the string became free and St John beamed as he reeled it in. Still attached to the end of the piece of string was the tail, but of the rest of the mouse there was nothing to be seen. Nor was there any sign of our kitten. The smile disappeared from St John's face and he rushed down the cellar stairs to try to salvage the situation. Eventually he returned carrying the novice mouser, which was looking smugly pleased with itself.

'So – we've got a kitten that can catch dead mice? That's not a huge step forward, is it, St John? I could bloody well do as well as that animal!' It was Arthur who expressed our collective opinion as we dispersed.

St John didn't respond to that criticism but instead whispered tenderly into the cat's ear, 'I think that's enough training for today.'

William had other plans for our cat and, for reasons best known to himself, decided that he wanted to test the well-known theory that when cats fall they always land on all four legs, no matter from what height, or in what position they start their descent. He performed this experiment in quite a scientific way, beginning by dropping the cat out of the ground floor window. Once he had confirmed the fact that the cat did indeed land safely on its four legs, he then moved upwards, repeating the process floor by floor. Finally, he dropped it out of a top–floor window, releasing it upside down. He proved his point repeatedly, for the cat landed safely and the right way up every time. Not surprisingly, however, it took some considerable time and a great deal of encouragement to entice the cat back indoors to continue its mouse-catching duties. It's possible that this was the reason that our cat never became a skilled mouse assassin, and preferred to make friends with our murine tenants rather than exterminate them. Now, as well as mice running around the kitchen we had a playful cat scampering about with them, which could make cooking quite hazardous.

Meanwhile, St John continued to insist that I should accompany him on his cello. He had discovered a book of short pieces for cello and piano, one of which was entitled *The Robots' March*. This was in the modern idiom and was never intended to be a melodic piece; yet when played badly on the cello accompanied by an out-of-tune piano, the musical experience proved to be quite excruciating. After a few performances before our housemates at PUBAR, St John felt that we were ready to perform to a wider public. I was still mentally scarred from my *Weary and Lonesome Traveller* episode but St John refused to take no for an answer – and at least he *could play* the cello, albeit badly. Our venue was to be St Thomas' Hospital, where there was a grand piano, reasonably in tune.

The music room was conveniently adjacent to St Thomas' House, and, after consuming a good deal of beer one Friday night, we were able to muster a small but select audience for our performance. About a dozen fellow-drinkers – including Frank, a friend of mine from Norwich who was staying at PUBAR – accompanied us, pints in hand, downstairs to the venue. I sat at the piano, and even as St John was tuning up, one member of our audience decided to leave, only to find that the door had been securely locked. St John had taken this precaution, knowing from past experience that it was unusual for an audience to want to stay for more than the first few bars of one of his performances. He was determined that, on this occasion, everyone should hear the whole piece played through.

It was to prove a memorable, if slightly painful, experience for both the performers and their incarcerated audience. I am still confident that when we began to play we both started at the same moment, but in retrospect I think what must have happened was that St John repeated a section of the music which I didn't. Whatever the reason, we lost synchronicity and as I crescendoed to the climax of the piece, striking the final loud chord with considerable aplomb, and then moved to stand up to take a bow, I was surprised to find that St John was still playing. I turned to see him, head down, vigorously stroking his bow across the strings of his cello. He seemed amazed that I had already finished and briefly looked up, muttering, 'Gosh, have you finished already? That was quick.' He still had some eighteen bars to go, but like a true professional he continued, and it was only after another ten seconds that he struck his final chord. With a dramatic flourish, he lifted his bow from the strings and stared triumphantly towards the audience who were by now looking distinctly pale. Someone at the back shouted out, 'Okay. Now, *please* let us out.'

But St John was not yet finished. He felt that we had not done ourselves full justice and insisted that we play it through twice more before he finally unlocked the door.

Back in the bar, St John and I celebrated our performance and then, along with Frank, Arthur and William, decided to go for a curry. We headed to Clapham and the Star of India. Not surprisingly, we were the last diners of the day. Curry-eating is a rite of passage for students and the rules are simple: you have to eat the hottest curry possible, without drinking anything cooling, such as lager or water. William assured us that the correct and authentic way to eat Indian cuisine was to use one's left hand and in order to facilitate this we all sat upon our right hand leaving the left free.

Frank was beginning to succumb from the numerous beers he had consumed even before the first course arrived, and as soon as it was placed in front of him he abandoned the struggle and fell soundly asleep with his head in his chicken vindaloo. Arthur tried to wake him by poking him in the face with his fork, but he remained wholly unresponsive and it soon became clear that Frank was out for the count. William carefully lifted his head while Arthur removed the plate. We shared his meal between us, replaced the empty dish and then gently lowered his head back on to the now clean plate.

It was as we were finishing our meal that the conversation turned to Bombay Duck and how difficult it was to eat, being so dry.

'I reckon, if pushed, I could eat ten or more of them.'

It was St John who said this, innocently enough, but it was a rash statement, at that time of night and in that company.

'Absolute rubbish! I bet you couldn't.' It was Arthur who responded and we all looked up with interest at this sudden and unexpected challenge.

'Okay. You're on,' and without further ado St John called the waiter over. Twenty Bombay Duck, please.' Then, to Arthur, he cautioned: 'No water, remember.'

The waiter was bemused but came back with the order and Arthur and St John began to eat.

Bombay Duck are a kind of dried salted fish, which smell rather like female genitalia, have the consistency of cardboard and are incredibly dry. Arthur and St John consumed ten apiece and, while both of them were now looking somewhat green, it was obvious that neither was about to back down.

'Some more?' Arthur looked at St John, who didn't even answer but just beckoned the waiter over.

'Ten more Bombay Duck, please.'

The waiter went to the kitchen to return with four.

'I'm afraid we have run out, you know. This is all we have,' he explained. 'No one has ever eaten so many Bombay Duck, Most of our guests don't like them!'

Undoubtedly this was a stroke of good fortune, since any more might well have proved lethal. With these consumed and honours equal we finished our drinks and wakened Frank, who looked with some surprise at his empty plate. 'Where's my curry?' he asked, looking around to see if we had hidden it somewhere.

'You ate it,' I said, 'then you fell asleep.'

'Did I?' Frank looked puzzled. 'Are you sure?'

'Of course you did. Don't you remember?' William added, pointing to his clean plate. It might have been the lingering smell of chicken vindaloo in his hair that convinced Frank.

'Ah yes! I remember. It was very nice. I feel so much better for that.'

Frank's capacity to sleep through the action and peak too early was something we would observe time and time again.

Soon after leaving the restaurant, St John and Arthur developed severe abdominal cramps and even having drunk four pints of water each they both found it difficult to straighten up. For about a week after, it was a brave man who went into the toilet at PUBAR after Arthur or St John had been there.

* * *

'Oi, you! Yes, *you* at the back.' I looked up. There could be no doubting it, *I* was the one who was being addressed. The speaker was the senior surgical registrar. Tall and slim, he was the epitome of a St Thomas' doctor. Viewed from the side, his face was convex, the smooth curve of his profile originating somewhere near the top of his skull. From there, the arc extended unbroken along his forehead, where there was some thinning hair, to his curved Romanesque nose, and then – with just a small protrusion in the contour which represented his vestigial chin – his face merged imperceptibly into his neck. This was long and thin and half way down there was a starched white collar attached to a bright red-striped shirt. The front stud was just visible below a tightly-knotted old school tie and his prominent Adam's apple made the tie bob up and down whenever he swallowed. His brilliant white coat was buttoned, but the top of his waistcoat was just visible, as were the turn-ups of his striped trousers below which his sturdy black shoes had a parade-ground gloss. This man was St Thomas' through and through; he was the very essence, indeed the caricature of a senior registrar, a consultant-in-waiting, within what was arguably the oldest teaching hospital in London.

I was at the back of a group of eight or so students surrounding a bed in which was sitting a middle-aged man with a red face and bloodshot eyes. 'Yes. *You*. Come here.' His tie bobbed up and down as he beckoned me forward to the bedside. My colleagues moved aside to allow me a passage through.

'Now, in order to save time, I'll tell you a bit about this gentleman. He's fifty-six, is a taxi driver and came into A&E

complaining of a swollen face.' Our teacher now looked directly at me. 'Now, would you examine this gentleman's neck and chest, please?'

'Hello, sir,' I introduced myself to the occupant of the bed. 'Would you mind if I examined your chest, please?'

'No. Not at all. Go ahead. That's fine by me, son.' The taxi driver's voice was gravelly and deep. He seemed quite relaxed and as unconcerned as if he were about to give me a tip for the two-thirty at Newmarket.

'Thank you. Would you mind taking your top off, please?'

'All right, son.' So saying, he unbuttoned and then removed his striped pyjama jacket. From his swollen purple face, bloodshot eyes peered through narrow slits. Over the upper part of his chest, full, deep-blue veins were clearly visible.

'Okay. Now tell me about his neck. What have you noticed?' Our teacher's tie wobbled up and down vigorously. I peered at the engorged, non-pulsating external jugular vein.

'What do you make of that?'

'His jugular venous pressure is raised.'

'Not just raised. What do you see? Describe it.'

'It's grossly engorged and non-pulsatile, sir.'

'Yes. Yes, absolutely. What do you think has caused that?'

'Could it be congestive heart failure?' I ventured.

'Possibly, but that doesn't really explain the other features.' Our teacher looked around at the group. 'Anyone else?'

William put his hand up.

'Yes, you. What do you think?'

'I think it's a case of superior vena cava obstruction,' he said confidently.

'*Yes*. Well done. Remember the appearance – once seen, never forgotten.' With this, the senior registrar turned to the patient, thanked him, and led the way off the ward to the doctor's room. There he turned to me again. 'What do you think has caused this?'

'Mediastinal disease causing obstruction to the superior vena cava.'

'Absolutely. Yes.' He then turned to Bill, who was standing next to me and whose mind had wandered to his plans for the forthcoming evening and the possibility of seducing his new girlfriend. 'What do you think might be the cause of his mediastinal obstruction?'

'Eh! Me?' Bill awoke from his reverie.

'Yes. You!' Bill was aware that he had been asked something, but was not sure what the question was, let alone the answer. He used a ploy that had worked for him in the past and pronounced confidently, 'Oh! The causes are legion, sir.' Our teacher looked him directly in the eye and smiled. 'All right then, just give me a cohort or two.'

Bill regained his composure and made an inspired guess, 'Some sort of malignancy?'

'Yes of course. What's top of the list?'

'Carcinoma of the bronchus,' I volunteered.

'Exactly. About two months to live, I should think. Now let's move on.'

As we walked along the corridor to the adjacent ward and towards our next patient, I found myself next to Arthur. He nudged me gently and whispered, 'Hey, Grahame, did you know that fifty percent of men commit suicide after having a penectomy?'

'No. I'd no idea.' I said, slightly perplexed by this *non sequitur*.

'Yes apparently so, I read it in *Bailey and Love* this morning.'

'Really?'

'Yes. Makes you wonder, doesn't it?

'Suppose so,' I replied as we reached the bedside of our next patient.

'Fancy a beer afterwards?'

'Fine. I'll see you in the bar.'

And so our apprenticeship continued.

CHAPTER 9:

ONWARDS AND UPWARDS

In the spring term William and St John decided to join the St Thomas' climbing club. After a weekend's rock-climbing in Wales, they were very keen, once back in London, to demonstrate their newly found skills and took to climbing into buildings rather than using the more traditional entry-portal of a doorway. I was personally scared of heights, but after a few beers would climb the side of a building with them like a ferret up a trouser-leg. Climbing into St Thomas' House was relatively easy and it saved us the five-shilling entrance fee to the student dances held there every so often. These discos were well attended by nurses who knew no better than to be in the same vicinity as medical students on a Friday night. As well as being scared of heights when sober, I was normally too self-conscious to dance, but after half a dozen pints the world was a different place. However, getting just the right amount of beer on board to ensure optimal dancing prowess, without adversely affecting coordination, required very fine judgement and on occasions I got the balance badly wrong.

Rose and I had an on-off relationship and on the evening of one of those dances I found myself unaccompanied. Once again I was dressed as Lord Byron and after a few beers with the boys from PUBAR in The Artichoke – a nearby pub – we decided to climb in to St Thomas' House. Apart from landing in the lap of one poor girl who happened to be sitting below the window through which we decided to enter, the climb was uneventful.

After a few more beers I spotted an attractive girl standing on her own and asked her to dance. Somewhat to my surprise she agreed. It was probably my over-enthusiastic dancing following so soon after numerous pints of beer that unsettled my stomach. I began to feel nauseous and started to head for the toilet – but it was too late. Violently and voluminously I vomited all over the poor girl and also a few bystanders for good measure. Girls screamed and backed away as I ran for the toilet. Some time later, when I had cleaned myself up, I sheepishly returned and was amazed to find the girl was still there. I apologised profusely and, though initially a trifle upset, she still accepted my invitation for a date the following night. After this inauspicious start, however, it was hardly surprising that the romance failed to flourish.

Thereafter it became *de rigueur* to climb into a social venue rather than enter by the front door, and barely a week would go past without us scrambling up some edifice or another.

It was Saturday night. William, Arthur and myself were enjoying a final beer in The Masons' Arms. The bell signalling last orders had been rung, yet none of us felt ready to go home. We were pondering what to do next when William suddenly said, 'I know! Jane told me she's been invited to a party tonight. Somewhere in Victoria Rise – number ten, I think. We could go and try to gate-crash.' Arthur checked his A to Z, which – like his collapsible umbrella – was never far from his person. 'It's just down the road. We could be there in twenty minutes.' Without hesitation we set off.

On arriving, things seemed remarkably quiet and in retrospect the absence of any noise or lights should have rung alarm bells, but after an evening's drinking in The Mason's Arms these warning signals failed to register. We scaled the front wall of the two-storey house and William, who was in the lead, gently eased through an open window and began to climb in. He was thus the first to step on the head of a man who, until then, had been fast asleep in a bed located just inside.

'Excuse me, but could you tell us where the party is?' William asked politely, while scrambling off the bed, and half-falling on to the floor of the bedroom.

The man on whose head he had trodden leapt out of bed. He was aged about thirty and muscularly built; his eyes were wide with a mixture of surprise, fright and anger, and he was wearing only underpants. 'Who the hell are you?' So saying, he bent down, grabbed a baseball bat from below the bed and, holding this in one hand, with the other started vigorously to shake a woman who was still sound asleep. 'Wanda, we've got burglars. Quick! Get up.' So saying he pulled her out of bed and backed towards the wall where he stood, bat in hand, with a bemused Wanda cowering behind him and shivering in her nightie. 'What the hell are you doing climbing into my bedroom? I'm going to call the police.'

A number of things were now beginning to dawn on William. Firstly there was no party there; secondly, he had just climbed, quite uninvited, into someone else's bedroom; thirdly, the occupants of the room were now understandably a trifle upset and about to call the police. Finally, two of his friends were halfway up the outside wall and at any moment would appear at the open window. It was now becoming apparent to William how the situation might appear to an unbiased observer, and the potential for a less than satisfactory outcome to the evening was looking ever more likely.

'Oh no! This is the wrong house – gosh, I'm so sorry – we're medical students – we were told there was a party here.' William said all of this in a staccato fashion, speaking with uncharacteristic rapidity.

The man continued to wield his bat, holding it in both hands. 'Wanda, go and call the police while I keep an eye on *him*.' Wanda began to edge along the wall towards the landing, where there was a phone.

It was at this moment that Arthur rolled noisily over the window-sill and on to the now-vacated bed. 'Hi, chaps. Bit dark in here. Where's the party?' Arthur was peering into the darkness of the room, and as his eyes grew accustomed to the gloom he noticed the couple standing against the wall. 'What's going on, William? Why's that man only wearing underpants and waving a bat around?'

Finally I clambered through the window. 'It's a bit quiet!' I remarked. 'Unusual not to have any music.'

Amazingly these inane comments, along with the strong smell of alcohol, had the effect of defusing the situation. We began to take stock and the awful reality began to dawn on Arthur and myself – that we had just broken into a private residence.

'Oh no! Shit.'

'It's the wrong house. William, you *idiot*, It's the wrong house.'

'Yes, I know. I am just apologising to this nice gentleman and his wife for our disgraceful intrusion.' William felt as though he was making some progress and that it was important to keep talking; so now in his more usual, slow and educated fashion, he continued his defence of our break-in.

'Look, we're most awfully sorry, but we've obviously been given the wrong address. We were told there was a party here.'

Arthur and I concurred virtually in unison. 'Look, we're most dreadfully sorry. Obviously we were misled, but if you could just show us where the front door is, we'll be off straight away.'

By now the startled couple were angry rather than frightened. The man was still standing against the wall grasping the baseball bat but his wife, perhaps more responsive to our pleas, had paused on her way to the phone and was hesitating by the bedroom door not entirely sure what to do. We seized the opportunity and all three of us slowly filed past her, through the open door and on to the landing, while simultaneously muttering, 'Wrong address. So sorry.' From there we could see the staircase down which we silently tiptoed, walking edgewise in order to keep one eye on the man and his bat, while continuing to apologise profusely. Arthur reached the front door first, and once he had opened it, with a final 'Awfully sorry! Wrong house,' we raced off into the safety of the night. We then sprinted along the street and took a circuitous route back to PUBAR. When William later accused Jane of deliberately misleading us, she explained that the party had been in another Victoria Rise, some ten miles away in north London.

Other medical schools were clearly considered legitimate targets for a bit of fun, and climbing into the Nurse's Home at Guy's Hospital must have seemed like a good idea at the time. Four of us – Charles, Arthur, William and myself – made the trip to Southwark and it was at about eleven at night when we started our ascent. The Nurse's Home was on the right-hand side of an attractive Georgian square, just inside the main entrance to the hospital. In the centre were well-tended gardens, surrounded by a wide pathway with benches on either side, where patients and nurses might sit in the summer sun. The building was a classic Georgian edifice of four storeys, with tempting keyed-in cornerstones, which made an easy climb.

On seeing the height of the building, Charles absolutely refused to take part, but he did agree to keep watch. Taking up his station on one of the benches, he then lit his pipe and sat there smoking nervously. The rest of us climbed up the edge of the building until we reached a narrow, rather flimsy ledge just below the top range of windows. With William in the lead we then started to traverse cautiously along, using whatever we could find as handholds. I looked down and became distinctly uneasy. We were about forty feet up, and, far below, I could see Charles sitting with his legs crossed on the bench. His head was enveloped in a pall of tobacco-smoke as he puffed furiously, trying to look as if it was quite natural to be sitting outside a nurses' home smoking a pipe in the hospital gardens at midnight. 'For God's sake, let's get inside, William, I'm not at all happy out here,' I whispered as calmly as I could, aware that I was beginning to panic.

'Here's an open window,' he replied.

'Thank heavens! Let's get in.'

Once again we landed straight into a bedroom, occupied on this occasion by a sleeping nurse. She awoke, startled to find three men entering her room, four storeys up. William rose to the occasion by explaining in reassuring tones – as if this were the most natural occurrence in the world: 'We're from Tommie's and we're just climbing in for fun. We're not here to hurt you; we just need to get out again.' This was not vintage William, and I personally thought it a rather lame excuse for a trio of men entering a nurse's bedroom, on the fourth floor, in the middle of the night, and entirely uninvited. However, unable to think of anything better to say, and hugely relieved to be off the ledge, I muttered, 'Tommie's men. Just trying to get out. No harm meant. Very sorry.' Arthur, who was last in, was still more lost for words and simply added, 'Yes. Me too.'

Amazingly, this had the desired calming effect and the nurse silently pointed to the door. We let ourselves out into the main corridor at the end of which stood a lift. To avoid the main entrance, where we knew there was a porter, we took the lift down to the basement where we found ourselves in a locker-room. On the outer wall above the lockers just below the ceiling, about level with the ground outside, there was a partially-open window which we decided was our best chance of exiting undetected. We tried to hoist William on to the top of the locker just beneath the open window. The noise was tremendous and it soon became clear that not only were we very likely to attract attention if we continued but were also having no success in gaining access to the window. Eventually we decided the only solution was for one of us to take a running jump at the locker in order to catch hold of the lower edge of the window. Arthur volunteered and after taking an athletic run up, launched himself with one almighty leap towards the locker. Unbeknown to us it was unattached to the wall, and

117

with Arthur still clinging on, it gradually and noisily fell back into the room, the racket only slightly muffled by the fact of it landing on top of him.

'For heaven's sake, be quiet,' I hissed in a loud whisper.

'Just *you* try and jump on a locker quietly!' was the angry rejoinder.

'Stop shouting, both of you,' ordered William. 'Somehow we've got to get out of here, before the police are called.'

It was as Arthur was getting up from the floor that we discovered the fallen locker was to prove our salvation, since it was now in an ideal position for us to use it as a step. One by one we crawled through the narrow window back into the quadrangle in front of the Nurses' Home. Charles, who was still puffing nervously at his pipe, having consumed nearly an ounce of tobacco, seemed greatly relieved to see us alive.

'Thank heavens you're back. What kept you so long? You made one hell of a row, and I think I heard someone coming,' he said, adding rather unnecessarily, 'For God's sake, hurry up.'

We walked quickly toward the hospital's main entrance, stopping only to pick up an abandoned stretcher trolley en route. With somewhat flawed logic, William reckoned that, if challenged, we could claim to be porters on legitimate business. However, no one attempted to apprehend us and we passed through the main gate without event. With a huge collective sigh of relief we ran along the road, pushing our prize and, stopping only to pick up two yellow flashing lights – which we placed on the trolley, front and back – we set off on the long walk back to St Thomas'. As we reached the centre of London, late-night revellers appeared somewhat bemused at the sight of us, but presumed we were involved in some form of student rag. It was only when we reached Regent Street and had sobered up considerably that we realised how conspicuous we were. We desperately tried to concoct a convincing explanation of why we were wheeling a hospital trolley with yellow flashing lights on it, should we be asked – which seemed increasingly likely.

'We could say we're medical students attending an emergency.' It was Charles who made this suggestion. The rest of us looked at him incredulously.

'*On foot*, Charles! In the middle of London? That's idiotic,' I said. The others agreed.

'Charles, you're a complete buffoon,' added William, 'Anyway, the lights are the wrong colour for a start. They should be blue!'

'Why don't we hail a taxi and tow it back?' Arthur's idea seemed the most feasible.

A few moments later we put this proposal to a taxi driver. 'You must be kidding,' was all he could say.

Accordingly, we abandoned our stretcher in a small side-road off Regent Street, hid the lamps under our jackets, where their continuous flashing gave us a rather ghostly appearance, and took the taxi home.

* * *

'Now, Mrs Robinson, tell us what's wrong, if you would.'

We were in the psychiatric outpatient clinic, six of us, sitting alongside the consultant psychiatrist who had asked the question.

'I've no idea. That's wot I'm here for, innit? For you to tell me wot's wrong.'

'Well, hopefully we can help. Tell us what you've been doing that you think is of concern.'

Mrs Robinson wiped a tear from her lined face. She was a rather dumpy, fifty-year old Lambethian. She looked about sixty, her face was deeply creased and grimy from a hard life, her hair prematurely grey. Although it was midsummer, she wore an old knee-length overcoat which had once been blue. It was missing several buttons and was now a variety of colours, spattered with the dirt and debris of twenty years wear. She had a cotton scarf around her neck which had once been colourful, and her lower legs were bare down to the woolly slippers on her feet.

'You're in debt. Is that right?' continued the doctor.

'Yes. That's because of all them televisions.'

'Ah! Yes, tell us about the televisions – if you would.'

'Well, I just goes out and buys 'em.'

'How do you mean? When your old one breaks down and you need a new one?'

'No. I just like buying tellies. I goes into a shop and buys 'em, sometimes four or five a day.'

'What do you do with them all?' The psychiatrist creased his eyebrows in genuine puzzlement.

'I gives 'em away.' Mrs Robinson was looking down at the floor while dabbing her increasingly moist eyes with a dirty linen handkerchief.

'To whom?'

'Friends mostly, but sometimes just to strangers.'

'Why do you give them away?'

'Well they're a nice present. You know.'

'But why do you give all these televisions away? Why do you need to?'

'Don't know. Just like to do it.'

There was a brief pause then the psychiatrist started his questioning again.

'Where do you get the money to buy all these televisions? How can you afford it?'

'Well, I can't. I just borrows the money to buy 'em. Sometimes I'll pawn one so's I can go buy another.'

'How does that strike you? Don't you think that's a bit odd?'

'Yes, I know. Sometimes I'll go months without buying any then suddenly things get bad an' I gets the urge and then I can't stop meself.'

'So are you in debt?'

'Yes. lots.'

'How much?'

'No idea. But it's a lot.' Mrs Robinson then began to sob, openly and noisily. Tears ran down her grimy face, leaving dark lines on her withered cheeks. Mucus bubbled from her nostrils as she tried to scrub herself clean with her dirty handkerchief, a process which only smeared the grime further across her face. I realised I was intruding on this pathetic individual's privacy and felt deeply uneasy. I thought the questioning should stop and my own eyes became moist at the thought of this sad woman who needed to buy televisions for affection. But there was to be no respite.

'What do you do for a living, Mrs Robinson?' continued the psychiatrist.

She made an effort to stop snivelling. 'Me? I'm a cleaner, so I am, sir'

'Are you married?'

'Wos.'

'Are you divorced?'

'No, 'e just left. 'Bout fifteen years ago it were.'

'Any children?'

'Yes. There's George. He's inside. And Jenny. Not sure where she is any more.'

'Doesn't she come and visit you?'

'Naw. Haven't seen 'er in years.'

'Do you have anyone at home?'

'No. On me own, I am.'

'Now, Mrs Robinson, I started you on some medication, some tablets, last time. Do you think they helped?'

Mrs Robinson looked at the floor. 'Never took 'em.' I'm sorry, doctor. I know I should 'ave but I never did, I'm eva so sorry.' She broke down and sobbed again. Her body heaved with the effort of her grief.

'That's all right. Don't worry. No one's going to tell you off.' The doctor tried to console her. More tenderly, he asked, 'Was there any reason why you didn't want to take the tablets?'

'Well I know I should've, but I was worried – you know – what they might do to me.'

She broke down sobbing again. We students all looked at the floor uncomfortably.

'When did you last buy a television, Mrs Robinson?

''Bout two weeks back.'

'And what did you do with it?'

'Gave it to somebody a few doors away. Deirdre, I think 'er name is.'

'Didn't she think it strange that you could afford to give her such an expensive gift?'

'Maybe; don't know, but she took it. She were right pleased, she were, as 'ers were broken. And her kids love it.'

'Well you understand the problem, don't you? You've bankrupted yourself by this behaviour. The tablets might well help. Would you be willing to try them?'

Yes, doctor I will. I promise. I can't go on like this any more.'

'Okay, Mrs Robinson. I'll give you another prescription.'

The psychiatrist started to write on the pad in front of him, and then, pen in hand, looked up at his patient, 'Do you mind if the students ask you some questions?'

'Nah, go ahead. That's fine.' She looked up as though this was the first time she had noticed us. I cleared my throat and looked down at the floor. None of us felt like saying anything. We were used to seeing the humour in most situations, but there was nothing to laugh about here. All we saw was just pure unadulterated sadness. Most of us were blinking back tears.

Bill cleared his throat. 'Where are you a cleaner, Mrs Robinson?' Good for him, I thought, for breaking the silence.

'Anywhere. Pubs mainly; offices; anything.'

'Thank you.'

More silence, then St John looked up and asked, 'Does anyone seem to tell you to buy these televisions, Mrs Robinson? You know, like voices in your head, that sort of thing.'

'Nah. Nobody tells me. I just does it off me own bat.'

The consultant tore the prescription from the pad and handed it over. 'Well, that's all for now, Mrs Robinson. Take the tablets and let's see you again in two months to find out how things are going.' He smiled benignly and gestured towards the door.

Mrs Robinson shuffled out of the room, her slippers making a scuffing noise on the linoleum.

As the door closed behind her, the psychiatrist settled back in his chair, clasped his hands in front of his abdomen and asked, 'Right then; what do you think is wrong with her? Any ideas?' There was a strained and painful silence. None of us really had a clue. 'Come on, you must have *some* ideas?' Bill was the first to attempt a diagnosis.

'She seems to have an obsessive disorder, sir.'

'Yes, that's true. Could be some sort of obsessive-compulsive psychosis, whatever that is. Any other ideas?'

Gerald was next, 'Could she be in a hypomanic phase of bipolar disease?'

'Could be. Any other ideas?'

'I wonder if she might have paranoid schizophrenia.' Arthur said with an air of authority. This was a cracking diagnosis, and we all looked at him, impressed. The problem was that he didn't know what it meant.

'Why?' challenged our teacher.

Arthur's lack of knowledge was now apparent and he hesitated. 'Well, I just do.' He said rather lamely.

'Could be.' The consultant psychiatrist then cast his gaze over us all, lifting his eyebrows as if asking for any further diagnoses. None came.

'Well it certainly is an extremely interesting case, I thought it worthwhile trying a mild sedative to see what happens. Well that's all for today. Thank you.' So saying, he put his pen back in his pocket and stood up to leave. Our chairs scraped and scratched as we all moved to stand. When the consultant was half way to the door, Bill coughed and asked, 'Excuse me, sir, but what actually *is* wrong with her?'

The psychiatrist stopped in mid-stride and turned, seemingly surprised at the question. 'Oh, I've absolutely no idea! But she's quite mad, of course.' And with a wry smile he left the clinic.

* * *

Once again I was short of money. After several fruitless discussions with my bank manager, I decided there was only one thing for it – to take an extended break from my studies and find a job. The spring term was mostly dedicated to pathology, which mainly involved classroom-based teaching. I calculated that I could miss three or four weeks, copy up the lecture notes in the evening and still not compromise my chances of passing the final exams *too* much. So, for the second time I went to see Stefan, the Polish ganger on the building site next to the Hospital, and signed up to start work as a labourer the following week.

CHAPTER 10:

THE KLOKOWOX

The following Monday, promptly at eight a.m., I clocked on. This was a time of day I rarely saw as I was used to lectures starting no earlier than ten o'clock. It was a beautiful late spring morning, the time of day when London is at its best, still fresh from the cleansing of the night, before the cars, lorries and buses fill the atmosphere of the capital with their raucous noise and evil fumes. I duly reported to Stefan and was given my instructions which were to work indoors, on rooms nearing completion. My specific rôle – modest, yet essential – in this massive construction project was to fill small holes in the plaster, preparing the walls for spray-painting. The tools of my trade – if you could call them that – comprised a flexible metal spatula and an old paint-tin lid, the latter serving as the palette on which I mixed the thick cream-coloured paste that was intended to repair any defects in the plasterwork. The only skill required was mixing the dry powder with water to obtain exactly the right consistency. Too thin, it would ooze out of the hole; too thick, it would cling to the spatula.

I found myself working on the fifth floor of the building and soon fell into the rhythm of an unskilled labourer's life. These rooms, now dark and desolate, would soon bustle with blue dresses, white coats, stethoscopes, cleaners and tea ladies; human beings of all colours, from different backgrounds and religions; the beds occupied by tramps, bankers, and street-sweepers, all laid out in neat rows. The corridors, kitchens and sluices would reverberate to the clatter of trolleys, sinks and bed pans, the crashing cymbals of stainless steel, while the wards themselves would echo variously to the sound of laughter and tears, the weeping of the sick and the well, the cured and the dying. Patients and relatives alike would play out their roles in the daily drama, the tragedy, the comedy and the miracles that are the very soul, the beating heart, of a hospital.

On the 17th June 1974, I was in the second week of my new job and had just begun work in the room at the north-west corner of the fifth floor, from where I had a magnificent, panoramic view across the Thames to the Houses of Parliament.

At exactly twenty-five minutes past eight in the morning the bomb went off. I'm not certain what initially attracted my attention, but suddenly a puff of smoke appeared above the Palace of Westminster and, less than a second later, there was a dull reverberating rumble. I looked across the river and gazed in amazement as the plume of smoke became a small cloud that gradually rose into the clear, still blue sky. Gradually it began to dawn on me what had happened – there had been an explosion – a bomb had been detonated in the *heart*, the very core of British democracy – the Houses of Parliament. I stood rigid, rooted to the spot, and as I struggled with this concept there followed an unnatural quietness.

Suddenly the silence was broken. 'Bomba! Bomba!' Tony – an Italian plasterer working on the same floor – had burst into the room screaming. He was running to and fro, pointing across the river to where a dense pall of smoke now lay above the Palace. 'Bomba! Bomba! The IRA – they bomba de building.'

'Are you sure?' I said quietly, continuing to stare intently towards the opposite side of the Thames. I was puzzled, seeking an alternative explanation. It certainly *sounded* like a bomb, but could we be certain?

'Si. Bomba, Bomba!'

'How d'you know? It could be a gas explosion.' Even as I said this I somehow *knew* that it wasn't.

Tony – who had become decidedly hysterical – now began to calm down, and from our prime viewing position we watched spellbound in the eerie silence as events began to unfold. We heard the first siren about five minutes later. That was followed by another, and then another, until the air was filled with their screaming. Police cars were the first vehicles to screech down Whitehall and along the Embankment in the direction of the Houses of Parliament, followed by a fleet of fire tenders and ambulances. Soon the whole vicinity had become a mass of emergency vehicles with their blue lights flashing, all parked at crazy angles, and surrounded by a carpet of tangled hoses.

We must have been watching in silence for ten minutes or more when someone, whom I didn't recognise, shouted that we should all immediately proceed to the ground floor. Tony and I accordingly made our way to the hoist where the others had already congregated and were listening to a transistor radio from which emanated the voice of Charlie Rich singing *Hey. Did you happen to see the most beautiful girl in the world?* Suddenly the vocal was interrupted and we all listened intently to the news bulletin; there had been a report of an explosion in the Palace of Westminster, the cause of which was as yet unknown.

We were all taken down to ground level, where we wandered about, chatting amongst ourselves and peering across the Thames where history was in the making. More than two hours later security announced that it was safe for us to return to work. Back on the fifth floor we gathered in the corner room from where we could view the frenetic proceedings across the expanse of water that was the Thames. Few holes were filled that day as the sirens wailed and vehicles raced up and down Whitehall. The news bulletins became more specific: a bomb had been detonated in the Palace of Westminster and eventually it was announced that this had been the work of the IRA. Tony had been right all along.

For the following week we talked of little else and later we learned that a twenty-pound bomb had indeed exploded in Westminster Hall. There had been a six-minute coded warning from the IRA. A gas main had been ignited, causing a fierce fire, and eleven people had been hurt. Amazingly no one was killed, but during that summer there were to be further attacks across the U.K. mainland, including those directed at the pubs in Guildford and Birmingham, claiming the lives of numerous civilians.

My day-to-day work was numbingly boring, but I developed a routine and carried a radio to help pass the time. I started work at eight in the morning. If you were more than two minutes late half an hour's pay was docked, so there was usually a small scrum of workers jostling for position beside the clocking on and off machine. Then we would all proceed to the changing room, which was a two-storey Portakabin – not that there was much for me to change, as I wore the same clothes on the building site as for lectures. A short walk across the mud led to the hoist where Bob the hoistman would take us up to our destinations for the day. Bob skilfully halted the hoist at each level, distributing workmen and tools, and I would disembark on the fifth floor. I often thought how strange it would seem later – when all the scaffolding had been dismantled – how I had walked in and out of that high-up ward through its window. One day I spied a small mouse cowering in the corner of the internal room on which I was working, and spent the whole morning wondering how it had managed to find its way there. Had it hitched a ride in the hoist with the workmen? Perhaps it had made a difficult climb up the scaffolding, or possibly it had crawled along the air-conditioning ducts. And having got there what were its chances of survival and finding a mate? Such inane questions buzzed through my mind, only to remain unanswered as I unconsciously filled hole after hole.

The solitude also allowed me to spend time – too much time – thinking about Julie. That had proved to be a disastrous affair. I first met her when staying at Simon's place in Brixton, sleeping on his floor, after I'd sublet my own room in Compton Cottage. She lived next door with some other nurses, including Arthur's girlfriend, Jess. I had always thought her to be unobtainable as she was so lively, engaging, bright and attractive as to be altogether out of my league. Julie had long ginger-red hair, a few freckles, an infectious giggle and a delicious figure. Consequently, I fell deeply in love for the first time in my life. It was during a party held in her flat that I asked her out and was amazed when she accepted. Over the following weeks I wooed her intensely. I bought her flowers and took her out for dinner; we went to the cinema, concerts and art galleries; yet I was always ill at ease. She remained aloof and out of reach. On occasions she seemed genuinely affectionate towards me, but at other times appeared wholly uninterested and unapproachable. This, of course, made her even more desirable and I became completely besotted.

Jess tried to warn me. She and I were sitting in the kitchen in PUBAR one evening waiting for Arthur, when she asked if I wanted to come out for a beer with them.

'Thanks, but I'm waiting for a call from Julie.' I replied.

She took the opportunity of this opening, saying quietly, 'Grahame. Has it ever occurred to you that Julie might just be using you? You know – going out with you while she has no one better?'

As I heard those words my whole world exploded. Deep inside I knew she was right, but to hear it said out loud cut me like a knife.

'D'you really think so?' I said, pretending that it didn't really matter one way or another. My eyes were moist and I looked down at the floor so that Jess wouldn't notice.

'Look, Grahame, I'm truly sorry to have to say this, but I'm not alone in thinking so, and some of us are a bit worried about you spending so much on her. We know you're short of money.

Of course, it's none of our business, but I feel I had to say something.'

'Well, thanks for that, Jess. I appreciate your concern.' As I spoke the front door banged open, Arthur came into the kitchen and so the conversation ended.

Though deep down I knew Jess was right, I couldn't bring myself to believe it and I continued to be at Julie's beck and call. I was growing more and more unsettled and as a result my behaviour grew less and less appropriate until eventually the inevitable happened. After spending an uncomfortable evening with her in a Brixton pub – where our banal conversation was punctuated by long silences – she announced that our relationship was over. I walked the two miles back to PUBAR, went up to my bedroom, lay on my bed, listening to the interminable announcements from Battersea Park Station – and sobbed.

I was mulling over those events for about the thousandth time, wondering how I might have managed things better, when the ten o'clock hooter sounded to announce our mid-morning break. Most of the fifth floor team had ceased work long before and were waiting for the hoist, reading their papers and chatting. Back at ground level, in a different Portakabin, we would buy bacon and egg rolls together with bottles of milk, which were consumed while reading a newspaper – usually the *Sun*. I had long ago noticed how labourers always folded their paper twice over into a square. Thus arranged, it fitted neatly into the pocket of a donkey jacket. That was one sure way of identifying a labourer or tradesman, the other being that they took their lunch mid-morning and their dinner in the middle of the day, at what I would call lunchtime. Many years before, my brother – the Woog – had been caught out by this. He had managed to find employment as an electrician's mate during the school summer-holidays. On his first day, our mother – the Zomp – had given him a packed lunch with sandwiches, a pork pie, a packet of Smith's crisps and a piece of cake. After a couple of hours' work, Bill, the electrician he was working with, announced that it was time to break off for lunch. Woog thought it was a bit early but managed to eat everything he had in the fifteen minutes allotted, while Bill just ate a biscuit and drank a cup of tea from his flask, amazed at his apprentice's voracious appetite. Woog only realised his error at midday, when they broke off for dinner and he had nothing left to eat.

During our dinner break I usually met up with Bob and a few others, crossed Lambeth Palace Road and strolled over to The Cut, a street in Lambeth, the whole length of which comprises an open-air market with an eclectic variety of shops and cafés along its length. The 'Shangri-La' was our destination. This was the café most favoured by the site workers and it was always busy at that time of day – being full of market traders, Lambethian shoppers and us labourers. We queued untidily, shuffling forward slowly until we reached a glass counter behind which stood the middle-aged proprietress. Her London accent could not hide her Italian descent and she directed the whole operation from behind a glass counter. An attractive olive-skinned, raven-haired lady, she usually wore a black short-sleeved dress over which was tied a white apron. Once she had taken our orders, we then sat on rickety wooden chairs, at tables covered with bright plastic cloths, waiting for our food to be served by one of the young waitresses. Normally I held back, at the end of the queue behind the others, so as not to make an error in ordering which would identify me as something other than a bone-fide labourer. I'm not sure why I bothered because my accent immediately gave me away, along with the fact that I invariably said 'Thank you,' rather than 'Ta.'

We always dined on something with chips – usually fish, or some sort of pie, often steak and kidney – along with a mug of tea and a slice of bread and butter. One day the Shangri-La attempted to become more cosmopolitan. I was the first to notice a blackboard outside the café proudly emblazoned in red chalk with the message: 'LASAGNE NOW AVAILABLE'. I prodded Bob who was standing in front of me. 'Hey, Bob. Why don't you try the lasagne for a change?'

'Wot's that?'

'It's pasta – Italian. You know, like spaghetti.'

'I 'ate spaghetti.' Bob was not impressed. 'I tried it once. It's all slippery and impossible to get in yer mouth. It just spills down your shirt and it all ends up in yer lap.' After a pause, he added, 'Stains yer clothes as well. Had to throw a shirt out the last time I ate spaghetti!' It was going to take a lot to convert Bob to a healthy Italian life-style but I persevered.

'I could show you how to eat it. It's quite easy. My Italian landlady taught me when I was in digs. Anyway, the whole thing about lasagne is that it's slabs of pasta and so doesn't slip off your fork. It has all the advantages of spaghetti Bolognese without any of the difficulties, and most of it ends up in your mouth rather than in your lap.' I was impressed with my sales pitch. By now, we had reached the head of the queue.

'Pie and chips, a slice, and a mug of tea please, luv.' Bob had not been persuaded.

'Why don't you try the lasagne?' the proprietress asked, her pencil poised above her notepad. 'It's Italian,' she explained helpfully. 'It's very nice, you know, and better for you than all those chips.'

'Ta, luv, but I'll have the pie and chips please, all the same.'

The owner of the Shangri-La sighed and took the order. Then looking up at me with a hopeful smile, she asked, 'Lasagne for you?' Although sorely tempted, I didn't dare let my friends down, solidarity being everything on the site.

'Pie and chips, tea and a slice, please,' I said.

I never saw lasagne on the menu again. Clearly, Lambeth was not yet ready for an Italian culinary revolution.

After lunch or dinner, whichever you called it, we would wander back to the site, go up in the hoist, and continue hole-filling until five o'clock when the final hooter of the day sounded.

Robbo was one of several Afro-Caribbean men working on the site. He was about forty-five and just under six foot tall; he had arms as thick as my thighs culminating in huge, powerful, calloused hands. He had a tendency to slouch and shuffled rather than walked, barely lifting his boots from the ground. Robbo always wore soiled dungarees and a stained felt peaked cap, which had originally been green and was customarily set at a jaunty angle on the back of his balding head. Although physically frightening in his appearance, he was as gentle as a kitten. A man of few words, he was the only one among us who read *The Times* at meal breaks, and he was working in what he called 'de deadhouse', a large room in the basement which would eventually become the mortuary. Robbo's pride and joy was his car – a battered, fifteen year old dirty-red Ford Cortina. On the rear parcel shelf he had laid some blue polythene sheeting on which were carefully placed a row of brightly-coloured plastic ducks.

One day, early during my sojourn on the site, I was on my way to the hoist when Robbo took my arm, looked at me with wide eyes and said, 'Look busy, man! De Klokowox is comin'.' I was distinctly puzzled.

'What's the Klokowox?' I asked.

Robbo looked shiftily from side to side to ensure no one was within hearing distance, then whispered in a conspiratorial fashion: 'No one know, man. He just come – unannounced.' He gave me one last meaningful, wide-eyed look, then turned and shuffled off in his characteristic fashion, as though he had already said too much. I had no idea what he was talking about and thought this was perhaps some sort of ghoulish mumbo-jumbo, a Voodoo-style apparition with a chalk-white face and a black top hat who visited those who failed to work hard enough. The Klokowox must have come and gone without my noticing and it was only some months later when I related this tale to Simon that I discovered Robbo had meant the Clerk of Works – so I judged myself to have been half-correct.

My unsatisfactory affair with Julie had left me feeling insecure and vulnerable. I was lonely, missed female company and badly wanted to speak to Rose. However, we had separated under circumstances of which I was not particularly proud and I felt both guilty and nervous about how she might respond to an approach from me. After hesitating for a few days, at the end of an excruciatingly long and boring day filling holes, I took the plunge and called her. On hearing her familiar voice, I said 'Hi! Rose. How are you?' After exchanging a few pleasantries I asked her if she would care to come out for a drink.

'Aren't you going out with Julie?' she asked, in her plummy, middle-England accent.

'No, no. That finished ages ago,' I lied.

'Okay. Where would you like to meet?'

Bless her! She was always there when I needed her.

CHAPTER 11:

PAY-DAY PHILOSOPHY

It was Thursday, and it was 4.30 in the afternoon. For the hundredth time that day I gazed out across the river, towards the barges moored midstream and the myriads of ant-like people bustling to and fro across Westminster Bridge. Directly opposite stood the Houses of Parliament, tall and proud, its fretwork of neo-gothic stonework bombed but unbowed.

On my radio Minnie Ripperton was singing *Midnight at the Oasis*, and the fifth floor gang were beginning to muster beside the window where the hoist would soon arrive. Those who had already congregated there cleaned their tools and read newspapers while waiting for the hooter to announce an end to the day's work. This was Thursday – pay-day – and instead of an evening copying out lecture notes, I was looking forward to going out for a drink with some of the friends I had made while labouring on this building site. Bob halted the hoist skilfully next to our window and rattled the cage doors open. As he brought us down to ground level we agreed to meet at the Two Eagles in about half an hour. Back in the changing-room I met another new friend, Nick, a law student who had ploughed his exams the previous summer. Unlike me, he was a skilled labourer and well-paid as a chippy's assistant. He took twelve pounds for every door that he hung, and there were hundreds of doors in a new hospital. Robbo was also in the changing room, sitting on the bench which ran its length; and whistling while undoing the laces of his work boots.

'Robbo, we're going out for a drink with Bob. D'you want to come along?' I asked. He looked up slowly, then pushed his dirty cap on to the back of his balding head and began scratching his coarse, grey, curly hair.

'You know I don' drink, man,' he said in that instantly recognisable throaty Caribbean accent.

'C'mon, Robbo, you can have an orange juice,' Nick offered encouragingly.

'No, man. I'm a-goin' home in my nice red car, with my nice ducks, then have some fish 'n' chip. *Goodnight.*'

Robbo hadn't taken an alcoholic drink since the occasion two years before when he'd nearly killed someone. He had been having a quiet beer, sitting alone in a nearby pub, and was reading *The Times* when a man who was standing at the bar and swaying perceptibly, called over to him, 'Hey, you.' Robbo had looked up. 'Yeah you! Can you read?' The chatter in the bar had immediately ceased. From previous experience Robbo knew what to do. To respond would only lead to trouble and, being black, he could only come off worse, so he calmly folded his newspaper, finished his beer and got up to leave. The stranger followed as Robbo shuffled in his characteristic fashion towards the door.

'You goin' answer me?' the stranger slurred, then after a pause added, 'nigger.'

'No, man. I'm jus' goin' home,' Robbo replied without turning round. The man followed, continuing to goad him, and for reasons Robbo could never later explain, he abruptly lost his customary self-control. This was not the first time a situation like this had developed, in fact it was quite a common occurrence, but perhaps this was just once too often; whatever the reason, Robbo snapped, spun round and let loose a haymaker of a punch. His tormentor, unfortunately for him, was within range, too inebriated to duck out of the way, and Robbo's fist caught him squarely on the left side of his head, felling him instantly and rendering him unconscious for two days. Robbo was charged with assault and narrowly avoided a custodial sentence. He had not taken a drink since, and we were not about to change his mind.

I changed out of my donkey jacket and joined the queue outside the cashier's office where I spotted Harry checking his pay. 'Harry! Nick, Bob and I are going for a beer. Fancy coming along?' I asked.

Harry wasn't his real name, but he looked like Harry Nielsen, the singer, and everyone knew him by that name. Aged about thirty, Harry was one of the many spray-painters on site. His overalls were invariably spotted with white paint and, though he wore a baseball cap in an attempt to protect his shoulder-length mane of light-brown hair, this was also liberally bespattered. He generally refused invitations to go out after work as he had five young children and was the family's sole earner. I was acutely aware that I was being paid nearly as much as he was, and with what to me was essentially beer-money he had to support a wife and children. He hesitated for a moment. 'Yeah, why not? But not for long. Mustn't be late home.' I was pleasantly surprised.

'Great! We're off to the Two Eagles in a few minutes. See you there.'

I checked my wages. The small brown envelope contained the princely sum of thirty-two pounds and forty pence. I transferred the money to my trouser pocket and briskly walked the fifty yards of muddy track toward the entrance to the building site where Nick was already waiting. As we crossed Lambeth Palace Road I glanced to my right, with a distinct feeling of guilt, towards St Thomas' Hospital where I should have spent the day in my short white coat – attending lectures and walking the wards – rather than in a donkey jacket on a building site. I was wary of being observed by my fellow-students, but needn't have worried, as they would all have gone home long ago. We walked the short distance to The Cut – where the stallholders were packing away their wares, while the detritus of a day's trading was being swept up by council workers – and then made our way to the Two Eagles.

Nick was a student but had been working on the site for some eight months. Although not a fully trained carpenter, he was allowed to work unsupervised, making a reasonable wage for a single man with no dependants and no mortgage. After two years of reading law at Queen Mary's College he had crashed out spectacularly the previous summer, badly failing all his exams. Rather than spend the summer resitting these, Nick decided to opt out and had been working on the site ever since. His father ran a moderate-sized firm of solicitors in his hometown of Cardiff and Nick's departure from full-time studies had led to a major family fall-out, since he had been expected to take over the business so that his father could retire.

Nick realised that sometime in the future he would have to resume his studies, but for the time being he was completely happy hanging doors, drinking and womanising. He didn't sound noticeably Welsh, but had an indeterminate BBC newsreader's accent, not unlike my own, and he was handsome in a typically posh sort of way. He had an aquiline nose and long, fair, straight hair which constantly flopped over his forehead. Every few minutes Nick would brush it out of his eyes with his left hand, in that characteristically public schoolboy fashion, only for it to fall back again immediately. It's astonishing how like finds like, but very soon after I had started my stint on the building site we had singled each other out and, chatting over a beer, had instantly sized each other up. The invitation to go for a pint was an undeclared drinking challenge. Both Nick and I were experienced pub-goers and, after some sabre-rattling with a couple of quick pints, each had recognised in the other a kindred spirit and there had been no need for either of us to prove ourselves further.

Bob on the other hand was a Londoner through and through. He had worked on building sites ever since leaving school at the age of fourteen, some sixteen years earlier. He had performed all the unskilled jobs and had been the hoist-man on the site ever since the building had risen above ground level. At five foot six, he barely reached my shoulders but, unlike me, who was slim to the point of being skinny, Bob was well-proportioned and muscular. The upper part of his nose ran parallel to his face, but half way down suddenly protruded like an iceberg, its natural shape having been rearranged following a fight many years earlier. His interests were philosophy – or at least in one particular Buddhist philosopher and writer – and dancing. Perfectly built for his preferred style of dance, the jive, he was a competition dancer. With his teddy-boy quiff, thick-soled black pumps, and long velvet jacket, our hoist-man would be centre-stage, or at least centre dance-floor most Friday and Saturday nights. He knew all the moves; his dance partner at one moment flying over his head, the next balanced on his back or sliding between his legs. I once asked him if there was ever any violence at these dances. 'Only at the end,' he replied philosophically. Bob's other passion was Lobsang Rampa. This Buddhist writer was an English plumber named Cyril Hoskin who claimed to have been reincarnated as Tuesday Lobsang Rampa. He had written a bestselling book, *The Third Eye,* and had a large following in the sixties and seventies.

Initially, when I started work on the building site, Bob and I had been somewhat wary of one another. He regarded me as posh, someone who looked down on him and the other regular labourers. I, in turn, felt more than a little scared of him, imagining from his broken nose and muscular build that he would be looking for a fight. One day I found myself sitting next to him during the mid-morning break. Cautiously, I'd introduced myself. 'Hi, I'm Grahame. Mind if I sit here?' and offered my hand, which he ignored. As I sat down he glanced at me suspiciously and then, looking back down at his newspaper, asked, 'You a student?'

'Yes.'

'What you studyin'?'

'Medicine.'

'What? To be a doctor?'

'Yes.'

'What, a *real* doctor?'

'Yes.'

'What you working 'ere for then?'

'I'm broke. Completely out of cash. I've had to take time out to earn some so I can continue my studies.'

'Shouldn't you be studyin' right now?'

'Yup. I should be in lectures, but I borrow the notes from a friend and copy them out in the evening.'

Hearing this, Bob stopped his questioning; his gaze softened, his craggy face creased into a smile and he began to chuckle. He extended his hand. 'I'm Bob,' he said as we shook hands.

Over bacon and egg rolls, we discovered a mutual interest in various different religious beliefs and discussed our musical tastes. Bob talked enthusiastically about Lobsang, of whom I had heard but never read, and sure enough next day he brought in his battered, dog-eared text and insisted I take it away and read it. I duly did so.

One chapter in particular intrigued me, and that was where Lobsang describes how to acquire the ability to leave one's body and travel through space – so-called astral travel. In the privacy of my bedroom in PUBAR, I surreptitiously tried to master this technique of extra-corporeal mobility. The Master had said that with practice it was possible to detach one's spiritual self from the mortal body and travel quite long distances, returning later to re-enter, apparently none the worse for the experience. I was particularly interested in the possibility of travelling the relatively short distance from Battersea to Brixton and thence to the house where Julie lived. I still felt upset by the break-up of our relationship and was keen to see her, even if only in spirit rather than body. As a scientist I couldn't truly believe that astral travel was possible and I felt quite embarrassed even trying to enter Julie's bedroom in this fashion – yet try I did.

I followed the Master's directions and for several nights relaxed on my bed and instructed all my molecules to travel into my toes and once there to have them fly out in a stream of consciousness. I was disappointed but not surprised when all my attempts failed and I remained ineluctably bound to my bed in PUBAR. The interruptions of regular announcements from the nearby station certainly may not have helped, but one way or another I failed even to make it out of the front door, let alone as far as Brixton. When I handed the book back to Bob and thanked him, I casually asked if he had had any luck with 'the old astral travel thing'. Bob admitted that he hadn't, and conceded that this skill was only achievable after very many years of dedicated training.

The Two Eagles was a traditional Lambeth hostelry, serving several different varieties of Young's beer, brewed just a few miles away in Wandsworth. It was a classic Victorian end-of-terrace corner pub with high ceilings and plaster cornices, all of which had been stained a uniform brown from years of nicotine impregnation. The bar, of solid oak, was to the left as one entered and an out-of-tune upright piano stood at the other end of the room. On Saturdays one of the locals would bang out such old favourites as *My old Man's a Dustman,* in return for a free beer; pints would be lined up on top of the piano, to be consumed between songs, and the room would be packed with men and women of all ages and infused with laughter, gossip; thick with cigarette smoke and Lambethian bonhomie.

When Nick and I duly arrived, half a dozen drinkers were already in the pub, mainly old men who had been ensconced there since opening time. As we were finishing our first pint, Harry and Bob arrived. Something I have noticed over the years is how white-collar workers dress down in the evening, whereas manual workers do the opposite and, true to form, both Harry and Bob had made an effort to look their best. Most of the paint had been removed from Harry's person and his dungarees replaced by smart brown trousers, while Bob was sporting clean jeans and a white shirt, along with a smart leather bomber-jacket. About their persons the heady smell of Brut aftershave was unmistakeable. I bought them both a beer and we all settled ourselves comfortably at a table.

Nick brushed the hair from his eyes, laid his pint down and, looking across the table at Bob, asked in his measured tones. 'Bob, what do you do when you're not driving that godforsaken hoist up and down?'

'Me? I dance. That's what. Rock 'n' roll. That's the business! Not only good fun but you also get to grab 'old of gals. Keeps you fit as well.' Bob was passionate about his favourite pastime. 'How about you, Harry?' Nick continued.

'I think it's important to keep your mind busy,' replied Harry thoughtfully, with less cockney in his accent than Bob. He then pronounced rather solemnly, 'Spray painting hardly challenges you intellectually, so I read as much as I can – and of course there's the cricket.' These were aspects of Harry's character that none of us had known about.

'What sort of things d'you read?' I asked.

'I'm reading Churchill's memoirs right now. It takes me a long time though, 'cos to be honest, I'm not very good at reading, and the children take up most of the evenings.'

'*Churchill's Memoirs*? What on earth do want to read *those* for?' asked Nick incredulously.

Harry bristled and defended himself. 'Why not? Important man, Churchill. Saved the country – that's all. Took part in the last ever cavalry charge during the Boer War, crossed the floor of the House, and led the Coalition. Probably won the war by getting Roosevelt involved. Never understood why he was booted out in '45.'

'True, but his books are about a million pages long,' I commented from the bar, where I was busy ordering another round of drinks.

'Yeah. But you don't learn anything without making the effort. You've got to make the most of your free time, I reckon.' Harry wanted to better himself and work his way off the building site, but was unsure how to do so, so he indiscriminately read whatever books he could lay his hands on.

'I think 'istory's a total waste of time. Should be concentratin' on the future, I reckon, not the past. Anyway, dancing's good enough for me,' Bob replied slightly defensively.

With fresh pints on the table Nick then offered his pack of cigarettes around. Harry didn't smoke, Bob and I took one and Nick lit them with his silver Dunhill lighter. After inhaling deeply he settled back rather pompously in his chair and blew cigarette smoke at the ceiling. 'Here we are, hurtling towards the precipice that is certain death, and all you guys want to do is speed up and run faster whether it's rock 'n' roll or spending forever reading Churchill's memoirs.' Nick always became argumentative after a few beers. 'There's an eternity of nothingness out there, so why not take time out to smell the flowers, relax and spend some time doing nothing. Have a holiday where there are no plans, nothing at all. Don't feel obliged to complete anything; that way there's no pressure and so no disappointments.' After this brief diatribe Nick brushed the hair out of his eyes once again, grabbed his pint mug and took a long draught of beer.

Harry was incensed. 'Totally wrong! *If* . . . ' he said emphatically, '. . . *If* we really are rushing toward a terminal precipice then we need to do as much as we can before we reach it. To get there and be peering over the edge into the abyss and thinking, bugger it, I should have done this, that or the other thing, would be the ultimate personal betrayal. You're just defending your idle lifestyle as a college dropout.' He wagged his right index finger in Nick's face to push the point home. 'Most of us haven't had the opportunities you've had.'

Nick put his now empty mug down on the table. 'Nonsense! As somebody once said, no one on their deathbed ever said they wished they'd spent more time at the office.' He leant forward and stubbed his cigarette out vigorously in the half-full ashtray in front of him.

'How do you know,' Harry continued, 'some people enjoy spending time in the office, away from the real stresses and responsibilities that they have at home.'

'Are you saying that work is less stressful than home life?' demanded Nick.

'For some of us, *Yes*. Certainly it is for me. I'm a spray-painter, right? I live in that high-rise block of flats opposite our building site with the wife and five kids. You never know if the lift's going to be working, if you're going to get stabbed when you to go in the front entrance, or if your kids have been offered drugs; now, *that's* stressful. For most of us, work is just a game. Very little if anything of what I do actually matters one jot in the greater scheme of things. Okay, I might make a mistake that costs the company a few bob, have to repaint a room maybe, so what? Nick – suppose you hang a door upside down. Nobody really suffers, but if you behave badly at home your relationships and your kid's future may be affected. And that damage will affect the next generation.'

Bob joined in. 'I agree with 'Arry. I reckon we've put the cart before the 'orse, personally. If you ask me, home's where the important things 'appen – not at work where nothing really matters. But wot do we do? We spend all our time and energy trying to do our best at work. A third of my day is spent asleep, at least a third working'. That leaves about eight hours. Some of it you're doing stuff like travelling, dressing, shavin' etc. The morning doesn't count as it's such a rush, so maybe you've got three hours left in the evenin' to do something with your family; but by then you're totally knackered and bad-tempered.'

'Or in the pub,' added Nick smugly.

'For heaven's sake, tell that to Grahame. He's hardly said anything. You saying that when he becomes a doctor it don't matter what 'e does at work?' Harry nodded in my direction.

'Nah! but someone else would do the job if he didn't, however there's nobody able to talk to 'is family as only he can. 'E's rushing to the – what d'you call it?'

'The abyss,' helped Nick.

'Yeah, – the abyss as fast as anyone, maybe faster. The only difference is that's 'e's mebbe doing something quite useful along

144

the way. That right, Grahame?' Now Bob as well as Harry was looking at me.

I didn't really want to be brought into the conversation. In my experience, pub philosophy always ended in tears. I was quite happy to let the others do the talking while I drank beer and let my mind wander. However, now *everyone* was staring at me, and a response was clearly expected.

'Sometimes I wonder.' I paused for a moment, hoping someone else would pick up the conversation but there was silence. 'I must say I'm inclined to agree with Nick. We're all rushing everywhere, not just at work, but in our free time as well. There's immense pressure to spend our time, including our leisure time, in the *proper way*, a sort of *designer* leisure, wearing the right kit and playing with designer toys. Okay, we have *more* leisure time now, but we're brainwashed into doing what we're *supposed* to do with it. We have to take exercise, not just to do it, but be *seen* to do it, and in a fashionable trendy way. So when we go to the gym, we have to wear the right kit. We have to cook like professionals and wear the right gear to cook in. Go to Regent Park any Sunday and there they all are, doing designer-leisure. We can't just relax in a passive way but have to be seen to do so in the correct fashion. We have to put on the right clothes to relax in; then we have to relax with the right mix of people. Multi-coloured and multi-cultural is good; and of course there must be at least one working-class person who is ostentatiously revered and deferred to, a bit like the village idiot in the past. Then there are all the toys – the gliders, the roller skates, the bubble-blowing things. It's all show; it's all bollocks, it's such useless time-wasting crap. And another thing. . .' I stopped for a moment after this outburst, and then added as a complete *non sequitur*, referring to the conversation of half an hour earlier, 'There's nothing more to life than life.' I stopped, annoyed at how much I had said, and lifted my pint.

After this outburst there was silence for quite a while.

'Wot *should* we do in our spare time then?' Bob was now genuinely puzzled.

'Something you don't have to plan or prepare for, as Nick says. No plans; so no expectations; so no disappointments.'

'But planning is sometimes the best bit, like lookin' forward to Christmas, or gettin' all togged up for a night's dancing, getting the gear on. Know wot I mean?'

'But, Bob, doing nothing also takes planning, so it's no different really.' Now Nick was deliberately obfuscating.

Harry tried to bring the conversation back on track. 'Back to the point – we have a limited time alive and we really have to make the most of it. I don't want to spend all my life spray-painting rooms and glossing windows!'

Nick looked him squarely in the eye. 'Yes. But what *is* making the most of it? Does that have to mean doing *something* – and if so, what? Or is it okay doing nothing apart from just existing?'

I offered my cigarettes round and lit one. The conversation was now beginning to irritate me and, as always after a few beers, I was now keen to expound some of my own ideas. 'It's the age-old question of what really makes for a *good life* and how do we achieve it. And remember, what might be a good life for one person might not necessarily be a good life for somebody else. Working the hoist and jiving is a good life for Bob; but smoking, drinking, and of course womanising, is a good life for Nick.'

'It's not easy spending all your life smoking and drinking, you know. It takes years of practice and consummate skill to do it with style.' Nick smiled and picked up his pint flamboyantly as though to demonstrate his point.

'Well said, Nick. Worthy of Oscar,' I chuckled.

'My dear chap, I know. Believe me – I know.' Nick smiled.

'You, Nick, are the unspeakable, pursuing the drinkable.'

'So we're *all* correct then? We can do anything we like as long as we call it the good life for *us*, because that makes it okay. I might like robbing people. Fine then. That's *my* good life. Might as well hit them on the head as well. That would be an even better life by your logic. Well, bollocks to all that.' Harry didn't usually swear, but he was now becoming annoyed.

I continued to develop my hypothesis. 'A good life is one that brings happiness to other people as well as to yourself. Bonking people on the head and lifting their wallets doesn't do that.' I explained patiently.

'Oh, so you have to bring happiness to others as well, do you? You didn't say that.'

'What about tonight?' asked Nick, 'Isn't this having a good life – or least a good evening?'

'Five pints and a chat? Of course, it would be an even better life with another five pints and some fish and chips.' I was beginning to get hungry.

'At least we're thinking about things and not just watching some soap on television with three-quarters of our brains switched off.' Harry, who had said this, always strictly limited the amount of time he allowed his children to watch television each evening.

'So what's wrong with that? If somebody enjoys it and it's harming nobody else, why not sprint to the abyss watching Coronation Street, rather than getting nowhere with a useless discussion like this one?' Nick was now being deliberately confrontational and Harry wasn't used to someone playing devil's advocate. He was taking all Nick's comments seriously and was growing more and more annoyed with them.

'You're so damn *negative*. It must be better to talk like this than sit and watch some rubbish on telly. Why d'you think I limit my children to one hour a night and try to read books? It's to better meself. That's why.'

'Oh, inherently superior, is it? Why? Just tell me why.' Nick continued to wind Harry up.

'Because by thinking about things, and discussing them, makes them more…' he hesitated, '. . . well, relevant!'

I joined in the discussion again. 'Well, it's all irrelevant, because none of us has any real control over what we do anyway.'

Nick and I had discussed determinism on many occasions – always after numerous beers.

'Oh, here we go again! I was wondering how long it would take you. Sodding determinism, from our doctor of sodding philosophy, Grahame *sodding* Howard,' sighed Nick as he blew a plume of cigarette smoke towards the ceiling.

'Yes! True. And that's because no one can successfully argue against it. As you well know.'

'If that's true, then there's no point in you becoming a doctor because what happens to your patient is already predetermined.'

'In a way you're right. Clearly we've no control over our own conception, or our embryonic development – which is all dictated by chemical reactions, so we have to ask the question when, and indeed why, we should ever achieve any control over ourselves or our environment. After birth, our infant development is totally subject to our five senses and interactions with others over which we have no influence, so why then should there suddenly be some sort of Pentecostal event, some sort of revelation, when we're suddenly allowed to take control of our own destiny.'

Nick smiled thoughtfully, 'If you follow that argument to its natural conclusion then none of us is responsible for our own behaviour, so my job as a lawyer – that is if I ever become one – is a waste of time as well, because criminals will claim that they have no control over their actions. That's clearly *rubbish* and could never happen.'

'Can you be so sure?' I said, raising my eyebrows.

'Personally, I think you're both talkin' rubbish. Who's round is it anyway.' With this Bob brought us back from our sophistry with a bang.

Nick reckoned it was predetermined that I should buy the next round of drinks. I smiled and got up to go to the bar. 'Proves my point, you see,' I said in a phoney Welsh accent, just to annoy him.

The conversation then drifted this way and that. Soon after nine o'clock, Harry decided he must get back home to his family and Bob left shortly after to meet his younger brother. Nick and I had nowhere to go and had imbibed too much beer to do anything useful, so we continued to smoke, drink and talk. At closing time we wandered to a nearby fish and chip shop, ordered plaice and chips and, in the gentle warmth of the summer evening, strolled back along the Cut, now quiet apart from the scream of the odd seagull scavenging remnants of food left from the day's trading. We chatted as we walked, picking our chips and pieces of battered fish from yesterday's newspaper. Past St Thomas' Hospital, past Lambeth Palace – the Archbishop of Canterbury's London residence – and on to the Elephant and Castle where we bade each other farewell and caught buses to our respective homes.

Nights like this consumed much of the money I earned, but there was always overtime on a Saturday and Sunday. What was originally intended to be a two-week sojourn on the building site became three and then four weeks, until a significant part of the term had been spent labouring. After nearly two months, once the acute financial crisis had passed, I decided that I really had to return to my studies. As a final gesture I painted, 'GCWH was here. 1974,' on the back of a lift-shaft on the fifth floor where some scaffolding still allowed access, and then signed off.

* * *

It was with considerable trepidation that I arrived at Lambeth Hospital the following Monday, put on my short white coat once more, and attended my first teaching round for many weeks. Some of my fellow-students asked where I had been, or whether I had been ill. Others didn't realise that I was supposed to be in their group at all.

'Just been earning some money,' I explained quietly, trying not to draw attention to myself. Our teacher that morning was the haematology senior registrar and as soon as he arrived I tried even harder to look inconspicuous at the back of the gaggle of eight or so other students. It was to all no avail. He asked my name and expressed polite surprise that I had been unable to attend his teaching round previously. He then went on to humiliate me by asking questions to which I hadn't the slightest clue. After about a quarter of an hour of this embarrassment, the entertainment value began to pall and to my great relief our lecturer thereafter ignored me entirely. Such was the teaching at St Thomas' Hospital Medical School – teaching by humiliation – but in this case, I had to admit, it was thoroughly deserved.

It therefore came as no surprise that I was second from last in the end of term pathology examination. The only reason I was spared the bottom slot and wooden spoon was that this highly dubious honour went to my friend St John, who had also spent the majority of the term on a building site – in his case so as to earn enough to buy a new bow for his cello.

CHAPTER 12:

THE CLAVICLE CLUB

In the following spring we residents of PUBAR decided to take up rowing. The head of the river race, or Hospital Bumps, as it was better known, is an annual event open to all London teaching hospital medical students. At the top end of this rowing hierarchy, the first eights from all the hospitals, rowed by the cream of student oarsmen (some of whom had already rowed for Cambridge or Oxford) competed on the Thames to be head of the river. At the other end of this spectrum of rowing skills, less serious but equally enthusiastic crews, like ours, formed social eights on which suitably colourful names were bestowed – such as Fornic Eight, Copul Eight, or Specul Eight. The last of these had nothing to do with the stock market, but took its name from the speculum, an instrument used to perform vaginal examinations.

We didn't let the fact that none of us had ever rowed in an eight before deter us in the least. If truth be told, I was the only member of our team who had any experience of rowing at all. While at school in Norwich I had joined the Sea Scouts and during summer evenings we would row a whaler up and down the Waveney River, past Norwich Yacht Station and onwards to warehouses, now long derelict but once busy when Norwich had been a thriving inland port. One year I was in the team picked to compete in the Boy Scouts' regatta on Teddington Lock. We were eliminated in the first heat, but this enabled those of us in the eighth Norwich team to fraternise with our female counterparts, the Sea Rangers. I persuaded one of them to swap hat-bands, starting a trend and soon all of us were proudly sporting SEA RANGERS emblazoned in gold thread around the rim of our sailor hats.

A whaler is a rather like an extremely large wooden bath, but with the water on the outside. They are sturdy, stable boats, ideal for transferring personnel and cargo from ship to shore, albeit at a sedate pace. A racing eight could hardly be more different – a streamlined greyhound of a boat, fast and disturbingly unstable. On our initial outings we were like children trying to balance on a bicycle for the first time. However, after a few practice sessions we declared ourselves fully competent to enter the head of the river race.

The essence of this contest is to 'bump' the stern of the boat immediately ahead or else have it acknowledged by that boat's coxswain that you have started to overtake them so that they are obliged to move aside to let you pass. If you didn't give or receive a bump then you had to 'row over'. That meant rowing the whole length of the course. As this was about two miles long and we weren't very fit, it was a penalty to be avoided if at all possible. There was therefore frenetic activity at the start of the race to try and catch the boat in front within the first thirty or forty yards. The races continued for several evenings so that a successful eight could move up a significant number of places during the course of the week's racing. Among our eight rowers, as well as myself at number five, were Arthur, St John, and William, rowing at numbers three, four and six, respectively.

The evening of our first race was pleasantly warm and balmy. It was late spring. The riverbanks and towpaths were carpeted with flowers, their intoxicating aroma pervading the atmosphere and overpowering the city smells; the world seemed clean and invigorated as nature was awakening to another year. The low sun cast a deep red reflection which danced across the placid Thames as we excitedly shouldered our eight from the boathouse and settled it gently on the water. We rowed neatly towards the middle of the river and then set off upstream on the two-mile journey to our designated starting point. Along the whole length of the course there was a distinctly carnival atmosphere and from the river banks and bridges came cheers of support from friends and evening promenaders who had stopped to watch the spectacle. It wasn't long, however, before our initial optimism was dampened as events started to go awry about half a mile from the start.

Even in perfect conditions such as these, the Thames is a dangerous river, with strong currents and huge variations in depth. We had just rowed smartly past a barge moored close to an island in mid-stream when we slowed and, with a gentle grinding sound, came to a complete halt. We didn't intend to – we just stopped. 'What's happened, Charles?' yelled William, twisting his torso round as far as he could to peer towards the front of the boat. Our bow oarsman, Charles, was peering with disbelief over the side where the bottom of the river was clearly visible barely six inches below the surface.

'We've run aground!' he shouted back.

'We can't have! We're in the middle of the bloody river! Look again.' William then recalled the time when Charles had first worn his contact lenses, injuring himself quite badly by falling up the steps of his hall of residence; consequently he and I had no faith in our team-mate's ability to judge the depth of the river accurately. But on this occasion Charles' contacts had not misled him – he was absolutely correct, for the bow of the boat was wedged firmly on a sandbank.

Our cox was a mature student called Jim. He was of diminutive stature, as becomes coxes and jockeys, and his head was barely visible above the gunwale of the boat. He too was perplexed as to how we could run have aground midstream in the Thames. 'Are you sure?' he shouted while trying to peer past the eight large oarsmen in front of him to where Charles was still looking unbelievingly at the bottom of the river.

'Yep. I can see the bottom clearly. We've hit a sandbank.'

'Can you get out and push us off?'

'I'll try.' And so saying, Charles stepped over the side of the boat and found himself standing in the middle of the river Thames in only ankle-deep water. He pushed and shoved as the rest of us tried to row in reverse but we were stuck firmly and it quickly became clear that he alone could not push us off the sandbank.

'She won't budge. I'll need some help,' he called out. At this stage, Jim – who as cox was responsible for our predicament in the first place – decided to take control of the situation and started to clamber out to assist.

'Right, I'll come and give you a hand.' With that, he half-stepped and half-fell out of the boat and with a loud splash disappeared completely from view. The problem was that at his end of the eight the water remained quite deep. Jim surfaced a few yards away, and still with a surprised look on his face remarked rather unnecessarily, 'Watch out, chaps, it's deeper at this end!' Then, coughing and spluttering, he swam to the sandbank. Eventually, after some very inelegant manoeuvring, we managed to re-launch the boat and, with all the crew back on board, proceeded to our allotted starting position on the bank of the river. We had now lost precious time and it was getting close to the start of the race.

The start in a bumps race tends to be a somewhat chaotic affair as the stern of the boat must be touching the shore – which at this point was of shingle – with the bow facing into the stream. This of course meant that the starboard oars, particularly those toward the stern, were on the shore or at best in shallow water. We had rehearsed the start on many occasions and the routine was to make three quarter-length strokes to move us away from the shore, then three half-length strokes to attain some speed, after which Jim, our coxswain, would shout, 'Lengthen', and we would all lean forward in unison for our first full-length stroke, and our boat would surge ahead at top speed.

This had worked perfectly well in practice, but the pressure of the occasion must have had an unsettling effect on us. When the starting gun was fired we successfully rowed away from the bank into deep water and, as soon as our cox called out 'Lengthen', we all leant forward as far as we could to deliver our first full-length stroke. It was then that Arthur caught a massive crab. Crabs usually occur when the oar is feathered rather than vertical in the water and, as there is less resistance than expected, the oarsman then shoots backwards – invariably destabilising the boat. In his enthusiasm, Arthur went one better and missed the river completely. He slammed backwards into St John, the oarsman behind him, who not only received an unpleasant surprise as Arthur's full weight hit him hard in the chest, but the force of the collision caused St John's seat to come off its tracks.

The seats in an eight have four small wheels attached to their underside and can thus roll to and fro on tracks or short rails to allow the rower to keep his oar in the water for as long as possible. It is therefore essential that all eight oarsmen slide up and down in unison to avoid either colliding with one another or entangling their oars. Maintaining this rhythm is difficult if not impossible when one of the seats has become derailed. Under normal circumstances we would have stopped, but this was a race and the boat behind us was rapidly closing in. St John did the only thing he could – he slid up and down the rails on his bottom. This was not ideal, because as well as being excruciatingly painful, his range of movement was significantly curtailed and considerably less than for the rowers in front and behind him. This meant that, as he leant forward with his oar out of the water, the handle of my oar hit him hard in the middle of his back just between the shoulder blades, while, whenever he pulled back and stroked his oar through the water, Arthur hit him hard on the chest.

We had a piece of luck, however, when the boat chasing us was itself bumped and thus pulled out of the race. The downside of this was that, with one of our eight oarsmen severely incapacitated, we were never going to catch the boat in front and so had to 'row over'. By the time we reached the bridge which signalled the finishing line, about twenty minutes later, St John was punch-drunk from being hit both fore and aft over two hundred times. There were, moreover, deep channels in his buttocks in consequence of sliding up and down the seat rails. It was some time before our housemate could sit down without a cushion, but the strength of character that he had shown on that occasion was undeniable.

* * *

It's amazing how quickly an event can become institutionalised. In a recent Old Boys' magazine I found an article entitled, 'The Clavicle', as though it referred to some venerable institution inaugurated several hundred years earlier, its origins lost in the mists of time. It had, in fact, been conceived by myself along with several other members of PUBAR, around 1973. This pub-crawl – because that is essentially what it entailed – was initiated one evening when William and I decided to patronise a few well-known hostelries between St Thomas' and St Bartholomew's Hospital. The students' bar at Bart's, we had learned, stayed open till the early hours of the morning. This quirk of the licensing laws was probably due to its being in the vicinity of Smithfield Meat Market where the opening times of local pubs – at two or three in the morning – reflected the hours worked by the traders. *En route* to Bart's we discovered a number of excellent watering holes and, along with a few colleagues, thought we would formalise this as a pub-crawl. Accordingly, one Friday night after an initial pint in St Thomas' House, we bade farewell to Ron, who was serving behind the bar, and set off for Bart's with the prospect of ten pubs to visit on the way.

The route took us over Westminster Bridge to St Stephen's Tavern, a cellar bar opposite the Houses of Parliament, then up Whitehall via another couple of pubs to Trafalgar Square where we visited the Sherlock Holmes. Then we strolled along the Strand to take in Hennekey's Wine Bar (reputed to have the longest bar in London) and so on to Fleet Street. In those days, Fleet Street was choc à bloc with excellent pubs catering to the needs of ever-thirsty journalists, The Cheshire Cheese being only one of several on our itinerary. It was at this stage that we sustained our first casualty. One individual from amongst our number, who must have taken leave of his senses, suggested that all eight of us should stand together on top of one of those large oval letter-boxes, the like of which I have not seen outside London. Perhaps rather surprisingly the rest of us agreed that this seemed an eminently reasonable feat to attempt, although in retrospect it was inevitable that someone would get hurt. That person happened to be Arthur who was the last of us to attempt the summit of the pillar-box. There he found that, contrary to our initial assessment, there was only space for seven of us so, after briefly balancing on the edge, he slipped and fell awkwardly to the pavement, somehow breaking his clavicle in the process. One of our group, who was in the year ahead, and had some knowledge of orthopaedics, astutely made the diagnosis by waggling Arthur's arm and noting how much it hurt him. Accordingly, he nobly volunteered to take Arthur back to the Accident and Emergency Department at St Thomas', while the rest of us carried on.

Two down as a result of this accident, we then crossed the road and decided we ought to hold a memorial pint for Arthur. This was to be a pint-in-one, drunk in complete silence as a gesture of respect for our fallen comrade. There were probably several reasons why we were asked to leave after less than ten minutes in this hostelry. One certainly was the fact that Charles, after successfully downing his pint in one, proceeded – equally successfully – to bring it back up in one, refilling his mug perfectly, right to the brim. The irony was that we were actually shown the door for being too noisy.

After this minor unpleasantness we proceeded along High Holborn, taking in two more pubs before reaching the Viaduct Tavern. Then it was on to Charterhouse Square and so to our final destination. By the time we reached Bart's we were, quite naturally, in high spirits and in a decidedly gregarious frame of mind, but we were then confronted with an unexpected problem. As we pushed open the door to the bar and our final destination, a fresh-faced student rushed up and asked us who we were. 'Tommie's men,' said William, attempting to push past him.

'Sorry, but only market traders and Bart's students are allowed in.'

'Okay then, we're market traders. *Now* let us in,' countered William.

'Sorry, but I need identification. It's the licensing laws.'

While St John and William continued to argue, I slipped past with the rest of our team and went up the few steps to the bar. I nudged my way to the front of the melée of students and legitimate market traders standing about the bar, and caught the barman's eye.

'Six pints of bitter, please.' The barman looked at me suspiciously.

'Traders,' I muttered. Astonishingly this seemed to be adequate for me to be served and the beers duly arrived. I carried a pint each for William and St John who were still in lively discussion with the student-cum-bouncer. I handed over their beers. 'Cheers, Grahame!' St John lifted his glass and took a large gulp.

'*Hey*, you can't do that! You're not allowed. *Stop*.' Far from obeying the bouncer's instructions, William followed suit and drained his pint. The futility of the situation was becoming apparent to the gate-keeper and after a gentle but firm nudge from William to get things going, the bouncer finally stood aside to let the three of us enter and join our friends at the bar.

There then arose the problem of our return journey. As we left the hospital and passed the site of William Wallace's execution, Smithfield Market was just opening and we walked over to view the proceedings. The activity was frenetic, as lorry-loads of carcasses were unloaded and carried into the market to be butchered. Arthur, William, St John and I watched the porters, with their blue striped aprons, blood-stained white coats, and small white peaked caps, all rushing about with huge sides of meat balanced precariously on their shoulders.

'Oi, you lads! What you doin' there, gawping like that?' One of the porters, a middle-aged muscular man with elaborate tattoos on both forearms, half a cow balanced on his right shoulder and a cigarette dangling from his mouth, halted and turned to address us.

'We're students and the bar's just closed,' said William, nodding in the direction of the hospital behind us, as though that explained everything.

'Oh, that's awright then. I thought you might be up to no good – doing a bit of petty thievin'. Know wot I mean?' The porter smiled, revealing his gums and a few residual teeth between two of which his cigarette was jammed. 'Come and give a us a hand then if you've nothing better to do.'

The porter introduced himself as Mick and he, along with his mate, showed us how to take the full weight of half a carcass on one shoulder. 'Wan' a go?' he asked.

'Yes, I'll try.' St John was up for it. He was headstrong and with twelve pints on board this was just the kind of challenge he relished. With a bit of help, he soon had half a pig's carcass balanced on his left shoulder and oozing blood slowly on to his tweed jacket. The rest of us needed no encouragement and soon we were all carrying pig and beef carcasses from the lorries into the bright lights of this ancient market where we attempted to hang them on the giant meat hooks inside. These carcasses each weigh forty or fifty kilos and there is a knack to lifting them, which we certainly didn't have, and so, an hour later, we bade our farewells, utterly exhausted and liberally besmeared with animal blood.

As we departed, Mick, in a gesture of thanks and goodwill, gave us some offal to take back with us. This comprised two kidneys (one from a pig, the other from a cow) and a set of 'lights'. This was in fact the 'pluck' of a pig, consisting of the heart and lungs together with the windpipe at the top. While we erratically wandered back the way we had come, along the now deserted streets, every so often I would blow into the windpipe so that the droopy lungs inflated and expanded like two purple balloons.

Eventually we crossed Westminster Bridge and, as St Thomas' Hospital came into view, William, who was carrying the kidneys, suddenly grabbed the pig's heart and lungs from me and sprinted ahead to the Accident and Emergency Department. Inside there was a reception desk, behind which sat the sister in charge dressed in her immaculate blue polka-dot uniform and starched frilly Nightingale cap. She looked up in some consternation as William pushed through the doors and rushed forward. This blood-stained apparition then proceeded to fling down on the desk the two kidneys along with the heart and lungs, and then yelled, 'There's been a *terrible* accident on the bridge!' William then looked down at the small pile of organs lying in front of him and with great passion said, '*Speak to me*!' and then, more loudly, 'Speak to me – *for God's sake – speak to me!*' and finally, after a short pause, adding, 'Bob,' to make the whole performance more meaningful.

The nurse first carefully inspected the front of her dress to make sure that no blood had splashed her uniform, then slowly and disdainfully looked up at William before pronouncing in a quiet and deliberate voice, 'You have precisely thirty seconds to get out of my department along with those…. *bits*,' and, gazing with distaste at the offal lying in front of her, she then added, 'before I call the police.'

St John and I were waiting outside and, as William exited the hospital carrying the organs, I asked, 'What's going on, William?'

'I just went to Casualty and put the organs on the reception desk saying there'd been an accident on the bridge. But the sister in charge had a complete sense of humour failure and threatened to call the police!'

'Ridiculous!' muttered St John. 'No sense of humour, that's her problem.'

I agreed. 'No sense of humour at all.'

'You'd think she might surely have seen the funny side,' said William with genuine surprise.

'Pretty, was she?' I asked, as we unsteadily wandered the rest of the way back to PUBAR.

Arthur soon recovered and the club was named The Clavicle Club in memory of his injury. We designed and commissioned our own tie, on the front of which figured a tankard inside which was a green C with a fracture line through it, while underneath was penned the motto '*Sine Cruribus*', which loosely translated means 'legless', although Latin scholars might argue the finer points of this interpretation. The pub-crawl subsequently became a bi-annual event of our sporting calendar, usually held in the autumn and spring. After a slight misunderstanding with the constabulary on one of those occasions, we were advised that it might be prudent to stay south of the river, where generally we had good relations with the Lambeth police. We therefore changed the route to make it circular, re-crossing the Thames via Southwark Bridge and thence back to St Thomas' through Lambeth. This meant that we didn't have the long walk back from Bart's at the end of the evening and also offered an ideal opportunity to increase the number of pubs visited to a total of twelve, thus making the whole experience more enjoyable – and indeed more of a challenge.

The following year we inaugurated our revised route, and were nearing its end when the bulk of our group were barred from a pub in Lambeth even before they had been served, just because one of them had vomited over the bar. William and I hung back, sensing trouble, and entered the pub through a different door. After reassuring the landlady that we had nothing whatsoever to do with the drunken hooligans next door and agreeing that the youth of today left a lot to be desired, we were duly served. The barred drinkers then congregated on the road outside, where some electrical cables were being laid. An empty cable-drum stood there on the pavement. It was about ten feet high and the last we saw of two of our group was the pair of them wrapped around the centre of the drum hanging on for dear life as it rolled down a gentle incline towards Waterloo Station, gaining speed all the time.

Back in the bar at St Thomas', William, Arthur, St John and myself were discussing the events of the evening and whether or not being barred from a pub disqualified one from membership of the Club, when Jess arrived to take Arthur home. None of us could later recall how there came to be a disagreement about the absorbency of tampons, but it may have followed what, at the time, seemed an intriguing debate about why they were eligible for value added tax when razor blades weren't. 'Gender discrimination, that's what I call it,' claimed Jess. Nevertheless I am confident that there was a good reason why William decided to test how much beer one could absorb.

'Definitely half a pint,' said William.

'Nonsense, don't talk rubbish,' was Arthur's confident response.

'Well there's only way to find out! Jess, let me have one of your tampons, please.' Jess dutifully rummaged about in her bag and produced a box of twenty from which she extracted one, and passed it to William. 'Here, Arthur, give me your glass.' Then, holding it by its string, William gently dipped the tampon into Arthur's half-pint glass. We all watched mesmerised as it expanded and the level of beer went down until only a dribble remained.

'There, you see it's all gone,' said William triumphantly.

'No it's not. Look.' Arthur took the glass, extracted the tampon and drank the remains of the beer. Then after unsteadily staring at the dripping item for several moments, unsure what to do next, he spun it round his head a few times and released his missile in the general direction of the far end of the room. The rest of us, keen to understand the aerodynamic properties of a beer-laden tampon, attempted unsuccessfully to follow its trajectory.

'Where's i' gone?' Arthur was now swaying dangerously, a bemused expression on his face.

'No idea, I can't see it,' said William looking around the room.

'Nor me,' I added as the three of us wandered aimlessly around peering at the floor in search of the missing item.

'You idiots, it's up there.' Jess, whose brain hadn't been addled by fourteen pints of beer, pointed to the ceiling to which the tampon was now firmly affixed. There it hung, like a large blob of bubble-gum, its little string dangling. The three of us looked up in disbelief. William was the first to vocalise his surprise. 'That's strange. I didn't know that was possible,' he said and then, to his eternal credit, decided to check to see if this had been a fluke. 'Here, Jess, give me another one,' and a second beer impregnated tampon made its way upwards, not to return. I decided to repeat the experiment and soon the whole packet of tampons had become securely attached to the ceiling, like small stalactites, far above our heads. Having exhausted Jess' reserves, of both tampons and patience, William and I had a final beer and surveyed the carnage within the bar. Bodies and vomit lay everywhere and we agreed that our new Clavicle Club route needed a little fine-tuning. The ceiling was far too high for the beery tampons to be removed and over the following weeks they gradually dried out and fell, one by one, upon the heads and into the beer glasses of unsuspecting customers below.

* * *

'So: pruritus vulvae. Give me a few causes of an itchy vulva.'

We were into our second week of gynaecology. It was Miss Summers, one of the senior registrars, who had asked us this question. She was an attractive woman in her early thirties; slim, blonde, with a handsome face and wearing a surprisingly short skirt. Her stockinged legs were crossed and a considerable expanse of this shapely part of her anatomy was visible from beneath her long white coat. All six of us in this tutorial group were male and the very idea of engaging eye-contact with her to discuss itchy vulvae was disconcerting.

'Well, come on. You must have some idea,' she said slightly irritably.

I tore my gaze away from her legs, looked up and coughed. 'Vaginal thrush?' I offered, and immediately felt my face flush. She looked directly at me and for the first time I noticed her startlingly blue eyes, which were now trained on me in a challenging fashion,

'Yes, good. Now what other symptoms would you expect?

'A vaginal discharge.'

'Okay. What *sort* of discharge would you expect?'

'Creamy or milky-coloured,' I hazarded.

'That's right. Well done. Let's have another cause, please.' Miss Summers turned her gaze towards the other members of her tutorial group. I began to relax, feeling I had done enough, for the time being at least. Her gaze rested on Bill sitting next to me. He responded. 'Skin conditions?' he said hesitantly.

'Yes, of course, but which ones?'

'Psoriasis?' Bill sounded more hopeful than confident.

'Yes, absolutely. Any generalised skin condition can affect the vulva. Now, some others please.

St John was next along the line and was staring intently at his feet. Usually barefoot, he had taken to wearing socks for clinical work but still wore sandals. He stopped wiggling his toes and looked up, 'Infestations,' he offered.

'Yes, yes. Very common, you mustn't forget them. Which ones?'

'Scabies?'

And so the tutorial proceeded. Having eventually identified the commoner causes of vulval itching, Miss Summers continued, 'Now, next we're going to see a patient and examine her vulva. All of you put on your white coats, please.' So saying, she stood and led the way out of the clinic room we were using for our tutorial, and into a nearby treatment room.

We followed her to where, lying on a couch, was a black woman. Her dress was pulled up around her waist, and from there down she was naked. Her hips were flexed and her legs spread widely open so that we could view her genitalia. The most striking feature, however, was that over her face was a small paper hand-towel placed there in a bizarre attempt to ensure anonymity. As she breathed in and out the tissue gently fluttered up and down.

'Now, this lady, whose face is covered for obvious reasons, has kindly agreed to let us look at her genitalia, so come along.'

We filed passed the patient's open thighs one at a time, looking with embarrassment at her vulva around which were numerous warty growths. Suddenly, midway through our inspection, she sneezed. The tissue over her face took off and landed some distance from the couch, revealing the features of a rather surprised-looking Afro-Caribbean woman in her forties. On seeing us, she gave an embarrassed smile while our tutor raced to retrieve the tissue and replaced it over her face. Then, anonymous once more, our patient proceeded to secure it with her left hand. After we had all taken a dutiful look, we mumbled our thanks in the direction of the tissue and returned to the clinic room.

'Now, tell me what causes that appearance,' Miss Summers started the questioning and so the tutorial proceeded.

A few minutes later I felt a gentle pressure from my left and glanced sideways to find Bill, sound asleep, mouth wide-open, with his head resting on my shoulder. Miss Summers – who had been listing the causes of a warty-looking vulva on a blackboard behind her – chose that moment to turn round. Her glance fell on Bill, who by now was snoring quietly. I looked at our lecturer and raised my eyebrows in a gesture designed to distance myself from his behaviour.

Miss Summers put an index finger to her mouth and whispered, 'Shush!' She delved into a drawer of the desk in front of her and withdrew a clockwork alarm used in the paediatric clinic to assess a baby's hearing. She walked over, put it against Bill's ear and then set it off. Bill woke with a start and in doing so lost what remaining purchase he had on his chair and crashed to the floor, sending the seat flying in the process. As the resulting laughter died down, Bill retrieved his chair and resumed sitting.

'Had a late night, did we?' Miss Summers fixed her piercing blue eyes on Bill and crossed her shapely legs in a slightly provocative fashion.

'Yes. Sorry. I must have dozed off. Awfully sorry,' Bill stammered, then he made the situation worse by adding, 'didn't get much sleep last night. Sorry.' A titter ran round our group and someone coughed quietly.

'Less nightlife and more studying. That's what you need, young man.' Miss Summers startling eyes steadfastly held Bill's gaze. 'Fewer nocturnal activities! Homework is to be encouraged but you do *not* need to study gynaecology *all* night!' She said this slowly as she tilted her head and raised her immaculate eyebrows to emphasise her point. The implication could not be mistaken and Bill's face was now the brightest shade of pink. 'Sorry!' he muttered once more.

'Well! I think that's enough excitement for one afternoon. Thank you, gentlemen.'

We thanked our teacher, filed out of the clinic room and headed for the bar in St Thomas' House.

CHAPTER 13:

A LITTLE UNPLEASANTNESS AT GASSIOTT HOUSE

I had kept in touch with two old school friends from Norwich who also had moved down to London. Bruce was working for a firm of accountants in the City of London; but it was Smithie who came to stay in PUBAR while one of the regular residents was away. He was the one who had put the plastic turd in my desk when we were in form one, and who in his final term at school had been responsible for the drug squad raiding the Senior Masters' common room as the Head was taking sherry with his colleagues. Smithie was studying to be a barrister and although he now wore a three-piece suit and had become prematurely bald – which gave him a superficial appearance of respectability – he had matured little and retained his impish sense of humour. His sojourn in PUBAR was to prove seriously deleterious to our studies.

The problem was that the bus taking us to our respective places of learning stopped opposite The Pavilion, a pub just around the corner from PUBAR. We were both of an impatient nature and unless the bus arrived promptly we would be tempted across the road for a beer and a game of darts rather than making the effort to go to our lectures. We became regular members of the Pavilion B darts team and on occasion even played away matches. This was not a particularly successful team, being second bottom of the local league. The encouraging feature, however, was that the team we had beaten by a small margin into last place was the Pavilion A team. It was after an evening of darts and socialising in this establishment that we unwittingly caused a bomb scare.

Rose had recently qualified and was now a staff nurse. She and one of her friends had moved into a small two-bedroom self-contained flat in Gassiott House, the Nurses' Home adjacent to St Thomas', where I had visited her on several occasions. As Smithie and I left The Pavilion at closing time one Thursday night, after yet another unsuccessful darts match, neither of us felt inclined to walk the short distance back to PUBAR and we were wondering what to do next. 'I know,' I said. 'Let's go and see Rose for a coffee.'

'But she lives in Gassiott House now, doesn't she?'

'Yes. We might even be able to scrounge a drink off her.'

'Are you sure it's not too late?' asked Smithie.

'No! Never too late to see Rose,' I replied.

'I mean, won't the Nurses' Home be closed?' Smithie looked at his watch. 'It's nearly 11.30.'

I hadn't realised how late it was. 'We can always climb in,' I said, and with that we set off in Smithie's green mini-van to drive the three miles from Battersea to St Thomas'. When we arrived we found that the large glass doors of Gassiott House were locked. Beyond these, however, a porter was visible in his little office to the right of the dimly-lit vestibule. Ignoring the bell, we knocked loudly on the glass and eventually this concierge slowly got to his feet and opened the door. 'What do you lads want?' he asked.

'We're here to visit one of the nurses.' I pronounced brightly with my most charming smile.

'Too late, mate. No visitors after nine o'clock. Good night!' He turned and began to walk lazily back to his cubbyhole.

'Couldn't you let us in for just a short time?' I asked desperately, as he turned his back on us.

'*Good night!*' was his unrelenting response and, with a nudge from his elbow, the door clicked and locked.

'It's no good, Grahame. He's not going to let us in.' Smithie was right and we were about to walk away when a nurse coming off duty – a frilly Nightingale hat perched on her head and a deep blue cape over her shoulders – rang the bell and the porter opened the door for her. With a brief word of thanks she bustled into the vestibule and as the door swung closed, both she and the porter disappeared into the dimness of the building leaving the door unattended. This time I hadn't heard any click from the lock.

I looked at Smithie and slowly walked back to the door. Pushing it gently, it swung open and without a word we both calmly walked through the entrance and into the vestibule. Once past the porter's cubbyhole we reached the main corridor which ran at right angles to the entrance. Here we darted to the right, in the opposite direction to that taken by the porter. From previous visits I knew that there were lifts at each end of the building and so we followed the gloomy passageway to one of these, the door of which lay open and bright in the semi-darkness. We entered and I pressed the button for the third floor. With a ping, which sounded worryingly loud in the quietness of the night, we ascended, entirely confident that we had escaped observation.

'So far, so good,' I whispered as the lift doors opened and we walked the short distance to Rose's flat. I tapped softly on the door. There was no reply.

'Try again, louder.' Smithie clearly thought I was being too timid. I knocked again, this time more loudly.

'Here. Let me.' Smithie nudged me aside and banged on the door with his fist but still there was no response.

'She must be on nights, or maybe asleep.' I said, 'I'll just leave her a message and then we'll get out of here.' I wrote a brief note on a scrap of paper that I'd found in my pocket and pushed it under the door. We then returned to the lift with a view to leaving the building as quickly as possible before we were discovered.

The lift slowed as we approached the ground floor and again there was that unnaturally loud ping when the doors began to open. As the gap widened and we were about to step out we saw in front of us the unmistakable outline of a policewoman. She was standing with her back to us, and on hearing the lift doors opening she turned and began to walk towards us.

'Oi! You two! Come here,' she said, quickening her pace.

For a moment Smithie and I were paralysed, but then as one man we jabbed the 'Doors Close' button repeatedly. With frustrating deliberation, the doors began to close but it was going to be a near thing and everything seemed to be happening in slow motion. However, just as the policewoman was reaching for the button to open the doors again, they pinged shut and our lift started to ascend.

'Bloody hell!' Smithie looked up at me. 'What on earth's going on? That was a policewoman!' Smithie's eyes were wide open and all the blood had drained from his face, leaving it ghostly white.

'I know *that*! What d'you think she was doing there?'

'She must have been waiting for us!'

'Maybe not,' I said with a forced attempt at nonchalance. Then, ever the optimist, I added, 'Maybe she's here on a social call. She might have a friend who's a nurse or this could be just part of her routine patrol, some sort of security check, nothing whatever to do with us.'

'You *idiot*! If that was the case, why was she trying to *arrest* us! What can we do?' Smithie of course was right. We were being hunted down.

As the lift headed for the top floor I desperately tried to remember the anatomy of the building. 'I know! We can cut across the roof to the stairwell on the other side of the building, and go down that way.' I said.

In the heat of the moment the obvious flaws in this argument had not occurred to me. Firstly, I had assumed that that there was only one member of the constabulary after us and that she would remain stationed where she was; and secondly, we still had to exit the building somehow, which meant passing the porter's cubbyhole. Nonetheless we exited the lift at the top floor and slammed open the door to the stairwell. We raced up the top flight of stairs and thence through a door out on to the flat roof. The sight that met us was horrifying. The clear starlit night was filled with the eerie brightness of blue flashing lights, and below us were about a dozen police officers of both sexes standing in front of the entrance to the building. If that wasn't enough, at least two dogs were enthusiastically straining at the leash while held in check by uniformed handlers. Our situation was not looking good.

'*Bloody hell!* Look at that. There's *hundreds* of 'em.' The situation had led to an entirely justifiable degree of hyperbole on my part.

Smithie on the other hand seemed to have lost his presence of mind completely and was standing stock-still, muttering slowly to himself, '*Oh Shit, Shit, Shit! Bugger. Bugger. Bugger!*'

'*Oh shit!*' I concurred, momentarily unable to think of anything more constructive to say.

We ran across the flat roof to the corresponding door on the opposite side and into the stairwell.

Smithie was first through the door and immediately muttered another expletive 'Oh shit!' and then more emphatically, 'Oh *shit!*' as he spotted two policemen on the landing below racing up the stairs towards us.

'Quick! Back across the roof,' I said and, stopping only momentarily to gauge the height we were at in case we needed to jump, I sprinted back across the roof to the doorway we had passed through only a minute before. I grabbed the handle and turned it. It wouldn't open; in the intervening seconds someone had locked it.

'It's locked!' I said incredulously.

'It can't be. We came out that way.' Smithie tried it himself. 'Bloody hell!' then, '*Oh shit.*' Our vocabulary was becoming distinctly limited.

I looked at the jumping option again. The design of the building was such that the main entrance – through which we had entered what seemed like an eternity ago – was in fact on the second floor, so that the drop from there to the ground could be only some fifteen feet. I was tempted by this idea, since once on the ground I reckoned I could outrun the constabulary. Whether it was because Smithie – who at five foot six and nearly a foot shorter than me – had further to fall, or whether his assessment of the risk was more realistic than mine, I will never know, but he was strongly of the opinion than jumping was *not* a good idea. I hesitated and the moment had gone. The police at the entrance below had seen us and were shining their torches so that we were caught in the cross beams, while others emerged through the doors to our right and left and made their way towards us. We could only do the honourable thing, and in true cowboy style put our hands in the air and gave ourselves up.

We were duly frisked, handcuffed and marched down the stairs. There, we were escorted to a visiting room more normally used for holding polite meetings between student nurses and their boyfriends than for incarcerating desperadoes. A police constable stayed in the room with us and, with the door now locked and the atmosphere growing less tense, he removed our handcuffs. Through the frosted glass of the upper half of the door we could see the outline of a policewoman on guard, standing at ease, hands clasped behind her back.

Some ten minutes later the door opened and a police inspector entered. 'I'm Inspector Cartwright of the Metropolitan Police,' he introduced himself. 'What on earth are you two doing breaking into these private premises? We know you were refused entry by the porter.' It was a reasonable question and I felt it was best to tell the truth.

'I'm a medical student from next door,' I said, nodding in the direction of St Thomas', 'and my girlfriend lives here, in flat 26. We stupidly thought we might come along to see her. We shouldn't have tried again after being refused entry. When we reached her room there was no reply and we thought she must be asleep so we just left a note under the door and left. That's when we saw you lot. I'm terribly sorry for all the trouble caused.'

'Any proof of identity?' the inspector asked with a sigh. I gave him my student card, which he studied for a moment then handed back.

The inspector then turned to Smithie. 'And you. Are you a medical student too?'

After only the briefest of hesitations, Smithie replied, 'No, officer. I'm a pupil barrister.' The inspector's eyes briefly narrowed.

'Are you indeed? Identification?'

Smithie searched through his wallet and offered his driving license.

'Any proof of occupation?'

Smithie searched again and all he could find were his Middle Temple dining cards and he handed these over.

'Those are my dining cards for the Middle Temple,' he explained. 'We have to dine there a certain number of times during our pupillage. You'll see they have my name on them.'

As Smithie explained that these were unique to him and that only trainee barristers could acquire them, I almost sensed a smile appearing on the policeman's face as the farcical nature of the situation became increasingly apparent. A policewoman knocked, entered, and handed Inspector Cartwright a piece of paper. I recognised her as the one who had tried to apprehend us earlier as the lift doors were closing. The two of them whispered for a while. The inspector turned to us; 'Well, it seems that the nurse in flat 26 does know you both and has shown us your note. Neither did she seem entirely surprised by your behaviour, bizarre though it is.'

The policewoman was more direct. 'We could charge you with evading arrest and wasting police time, as well as with illegal entry.' Smithie, who knew about such things, simply said, 'I know. Sorry.' We both hung our heads.

The tension was now relieved; the blue flashing lights and the dogs had gone. Smithie's dining cards had clinched our release. I had been fully expecting to spend another night in jail, but we were merely given a firm ticking-off and warned about the seriousness of wasting police time. Suitably contrite, we were then escorted from the building and released.

Later we learned that the porter had seen us enter the lift and had immediately contacted the police. The whole affair had escalated into a major incident on account of the heightened state of alert following the IRA bombing campaign. The fact that Gassiott House was an all-female Nurses' Home just opposite the Houses of Parliament meant that it was in a high-priority category for police protection.

As we walked past the front of the building where an hour earlier blue lights had been flashing and dogs barking, I gazed up at the roof on which we had been cornered, 'I *could* have jumped that.' I said to myself as much as to Smithie.

'You would have killed yourself!' Then he added, 'Strewth! That was close.'

We were now both stone-cold sober and ashen pale. Wisely deciding to leave the car where it was, we walked briskly away from the scene of the crime and, once out of sight of Gassiott House, spontaneously broke into a run which we maintained until we reached Battersea.

Next day there was much whispered gossip about a break-in at Gassiott House, followed by a police raid when a gang of desperadoes had tried to take some nurses hostage. Rose – bless her heart – thought the whole episode hilarious, but kept quiet to protect Smithie and me from trouble with our respective training authorities, who would most certainly have taken a very dim view of the whole escapade.

* * *

'Mr Arbuthnot? I enquired, as I approached the bed. The man I was addressing looked up. 'Yes. That's me.'

'Hi! My name's Grahame Howard and I'm a medical student. Would it be all right if I asked you a few questions and then examined you?'

'Fine. Go ahead. I've been expecting a visit from one of you chaps.' With that, Thomas Arbuthnot folded the newspaper he had been reading and placed it neatly on the locker beside his bed. He was a handsome, thirty-eight year old, well-proportioned and in his prime. Muscular without being brawny, he had a dark, good-looking, almost swarthy face and his short hair was just beginning to thin at the front. He was not wearing pyjama tops and over his well-developed pectoral muscles was a thatch of black hair.

After shaking his hand, I sat down beside the bed, and with pen and notepad ready started upon my well-rehearsed history-taking routine. 'Could you tell what the problem was that brought you into hospital?' I looked up from my pad expectantly. His dark eyes were bright and intelligent, yet he seemed quite unconcerned about his situation. 'Yes, nothing serious luckily, or so I gather, but I was playing tennis last week at the local club and the next day I noticed my left leg had swollen a little. Just the lower part, you know, near the ankle. I put it down to a minor injury from the game, a slight muscle tear – or something like that. But it grew steadily worse with the swelling extending right up to the knee, so after about two days I thought I should go to see my GP. It took a few days to get an appointment but I saw him last Friday. He took one look at my leg, which by then was swollen right up to the thigh, and sent me here immediately and I've been here ever since.'

'Right. That was three days ago then?' I finished what I was writing, and then looked at him again. 'Can you tell me what's happened since your admission?'

'Yes, I had an X-ray test – a venogram I think it's called – when I arrived and they told me I had a blood clot in my leg, which apparently is quite common. So they started me on blood-thinning treatment. I had injections at first, and then this morning I was started on the dreaded rat poison.' He smiled and looked at me.

'Ah yes.' I grinned back, 'that's the warfarin. Any improvement so far?'

'No. Not yet, but seemingly it will get better soon, and hopefully I'll be out of here in a day or two.'

I asked a few more questions and ascertained that he was an insurance broker, was married with two children, a girl aged seven and boy of three. He had always been fit in the past. Having finished my history-taking I put the pad down and, replacing my pen in the breast pocket of the slightly grubby short white coat I was wearing, asked, 'May I examine you now?'

He nodded consent and I pulled the curtains around his bed. I went through the whole examination procedure that we had been taught: cardiovascular, respiratory, gastro-intestinal and neurological systems – all in order. Finally I looked at his legs. His left leg was twice the size of the right; the skin was dark and dusky purple, while on his swollen ankle were a few flakes of loose skin rather like dandruff. I gently examined his groin and leg, felt for the pulses, and asked if it was painful behind his calf. Then, having finished, I pulled the covers back over his lower body.

'Thanks very much,' I said. 'Do you know what is going to happen now?'

'Well they need to get the dose of the rat poison right and I think I am having a test done on my abdomen this afternoon. No idea why.'

'Yes, that's routine. I'll be taking your blood tomorrow morning, I'll see you then.' We shook hands again and, with a cheery relaxed smile, he turned to pick his newspaper up and resume his reading.

When I came back the following day the patient whom I approached had changed beyond all recognition. Physically, he looked much the same but something was very different. I began with a smile. 'Good morning! Can I take some blood from you, please?' He didn't smile in response but simply held out his arm. I put a tourniquet around his upper arm and, having identified a suitable vein, punctured it and withdrew a syringe full of blood. I then set about filling the four small colour-coded bottles that I had lined up in readiness on the bedside cabinet. As well as routine blood tests of liver and renal function, one of the specimens was specifically for assessing whether or not the dose of warfarin was correct. Too much, and the patient was liable to bleed uncontrollably, too little and the blood clot would spread and could prove fatal. With the lids screwed back on to their bottles and having given them a little shake I made ready to leave. As I made a final check of the puncture site to ensure that it had stopped bleeding, I looked at him. His eyes were red and his face was more lined than the day before.

'How are you feeling?' I asked. For a moment he was silent and then he slowly turned his head to look at me.

'I was told the result of my scan yesterday. It seems I've got cancer. It's in the pancreas and has spread to my liver.' He hesitated; his lips trembled and tears filled his eyes. 'Apparently . . .' and here he paused to wipe his eyes . . . 'it seems I've only got a few months to live.' He rushed those last words in order to finish his sentence before breaking down; then his head fell forward, his shoulders heaved and he cried, the tears streaming down his face.

Between the sobs, he stammered, 'I'm sorry.' Then again, 'I'm sorry. But I just don't know what to do. I was playing tennis only last week and now I'm going to die! What'll I tell my wife and the kids? They're due in soon to see the doctor. Lucy's only seven. What'll they do without me? It's not fair. I'm only thirty-eight and I've just been promoted. It's simply not *fair*.'

I blinked my own tears back. I had no idea how to behave in this situation and didn't know what to say. We hadn't ever been taught what to do under such circumstances. It seemed slightly unnatural to hold another man's hand – but that's what I did. He grasped it tightly and squeezed while his whole body shook, racked with sobs. I didn't know what to do or say. We hadn't had a lecture on how to manage emotional situations like this, so I remained silent for a moment or two before whispering, 'I'm so sorry.' Hearing this, he grasped my hand more tightly then, as quickly as he had broken down and succumbed to his fear and sadness, he started to pull himself together.

'I'm sorry. I shouldn't have behaved like that. It's not what we chaps do, is it?' He smiled wryly. 'It's all come as such a shock.' He looked at me directly. For the first time in my life, I found myself looking into the eyes of someone who knew he would soon be dead. I wanted to look away but couldn't, for I knew instinctively that it would be the wrong thing to do.

'Thanks. Thanks for listening.' He released my hand and his smile deepened. 'You're a nice young man; I'm sure you'll make a good doctor. Good luck with your studies. Now, here comes my wife.' I looked down the ward to where the surgical registrar was striding towards us, unlit pipe in his mouth, accompanied by a terrified-looking woman with her daughter trailing behind. I shook Thomas Arbuthnot's hand as I slipped away and, with a final backward glance while the curtains were being drawn around his bed, walked slowly off the ward.

Instead of going directly to St Thomas' House, I stepped out into the fresh air and sunlight and walked to the west side of the Hospital. There I could be alone with my thoughts and, as I looked out over the rippling Thames from the busy, bustling, hurrying figures on the Embankment across to the Houses of Parliament my personal problems and concerns vanished into insignificance.

CHAPTER 14:

SOJOURN IN SOHO: AND THE PRICE OF SEX

Another friend from my schooldays, in Norwich, with whom I had kept in touch, was Bruce. He was now a trainee accountant working for a firm in the City and, like Smithie, had developed a superficial veneer of respectability which quickly evaporated after a beer or two. He was sporty, muscular and handsome, with short wiry hair and a slight stammer when nervous. A man of action rather than words, he was always in the vanguard of any adventure, at the very epicentre of an incident. The only problem was that he didn't always stop to consider the consequences of his actions. Bruce was the person who, one Christmas, had thought that turkey-plucking would be a good money-making scheme, a gambit which had traumatised us both, mentally as well as physically, and nearly led to our early demise from hypothermia. If there was a bad idea being considered, it invariably emanated from Bruce.

After the little unpleasantness at Gassiott House, I decided to keep my head down and stay out of trouble. So with my final exams now on the horizon I thought it would be sensible, and indeed safer, if I spent my evenings studying. However, when Bruce phoned one evening suggesting we meet for a few beers the following Friday, this seemed an entirely reasonable and welcome diversion. We agreed to rendezvous at a pub on Wardour Street in the heart of Soho, a district of London better known for its strip clubs and massage parlours than for its many excellent hostelries. We met at about six o'clock and, after an initial pint, strolled around Soho gazing at the garish neon signs and the pictures of unclad women with steatopygous buttocks and enormous breasts, contorting themselves in ways I found difficult to believe were physically possible.

We were sitting in our third pub of the evening, discussing the narrow escape Smithie and I had experienced at Gassiott House, when there came a sudden lull in the conversation. 'I wonder how much it costs?' Bruce asked, more to himself than to me. I glanced towards him and noticed that he seemed to be in a trance-like state, his pint glass held halfway between mouth and table, while his eyes rested vacantly on a red neon sign which could be seen through the window. I followed his gaze to the large bright letters spelling out: 'SEX'.

'What? To have sex?' I asked.

'Yes – you know – with a prostitute.'

'I've no idea,' I answered, 'but there's one way to find out. Ask one.'

'No. I couldn't possibly do that. Let's have another beer – my round, I think.'

It must have been the latent accountant within him but, as the evening wore on and more beer was consumed, Bruce grew increasingly obsessed and inquisitive about the market price of sex. A little later, while strolling between pubs, we passed the entrance to a Men Only club, and Bruce sidled up to the doorman to ask him the cost of entry. I stood well back and on his return asked, 'Well, what did he say, Bruce?'

'Just a Strip Club apparently,' he replied. 'Bloody expensive though! It's five pounds just to get in! Lord knows how much a beer would cost.'

We walked on to a brightly-lit doorway above which a flashing neon sign simply read: 'MASSAGE'. We stopped and peered inside.

'Over there! Look!' said Bruce excitedly. 'There's a price list. Let's go and have a peek.'

Half a dozen beers had reduced our inhibitions significantly and we needed no further encouragement to step through the invitingly open doors. In front of us, seated at a desk, was an attractive girl gazing idly at a magazine; behind her on the wall was the price list, rather like the menu on a blackboard in a cheap café. We were both peering at this when the girl raised her eyes and asked, 'What are you after, boys?' I turned to look at her. On closer inspection she was rather older than at first appeared, had reddish hair and a thick layer of makeup to match. She was now staring intently at me and I was becoming a trifle unnerved.

'We were just wondering what was on offer,' I said, trying to sound nonchalant, as though I were a seasoned customer comparing establishments.

'*And* the prices,' added Bruce, who seemed quite unconcerned and was still gazing at the board. 'Why is the relief massage more expensive than the whole-body one?' he asked naïvely, turning towards the receptionist. A reasonable enough question, I thought, but the girl was obviously not of the same opinion.

'Are you two taking the piss?' she snapped. Her eyes were suddenly hard and challenging and she fixed her hostile gaze first on me and then on Bruce.

'No – no! Not at all! We were just wondering. That's all.' I was beginning to panic.

'Look, boys, I don't know where you're from or what you're doing here but you're messing me about. If you're wise you'll *shove off.*' As she delivered this piece of advice she glanced toward a large black man who was standing near the doorway to the main establishment. He was wearing an ill-fitting silver-coloured suit which was far too small for his muscular build and was studying his highly polished shoes, hands clasped behind his back. Reluctantly he lifted his gaze from the floor and turned to look at us before saying in a deep but strangely quiet voice, 'You better leave, lads.' This was clearly non-negotiable.

'Sorry. Just interested, that's all,' I said meekly, as we both turned to leave. This proved to be just the first of several such premises from which we were to be ejected that night.

We strolled on through the dark night split by the greens and reds of flashing neon; mixing with tourists and sex-seekers while dodging kerb-crawling cars.

'Grahame,' asked Bruce. 'I really *do* wonder how much a prostitute would cost. Have you *any* idea?' He had no intention of hiring one, but was still intent on finding out and was becoming frustrated by our lack of progress.

'Look, Bruce. I've absolutely no idea. You could always ask though.' Saying this, I nodded toward a girl apparently standing on her own near the entrance to a club. It was clear to me that she was a tourist. She was dressed sensibly and what I took to be her boyfriend was standing just a few yards away, talking to the bouncer.

'D'you think I should?' asked Bruce.

'Yeah. Go and ask,' I responded wickedly, not believing for a moment that he would actually approach the girl. I was therefore quite dumbfounded when Bruce, after a moment's hesitation, walked straight up to her, bent his head forward, and whispered into her ear, 'How much?'

As soon as I realised that he was actually going to ask this respectable tourist out with her boyfriend how much she wanted for sex, I sensed trouble looming and began to drift along the street in the opposite direction.

Meanwhile the girl's response to Bruce's question was not quite what he had anticipated.

'How much *what*?' she said. Then after the briefest of pauses her eyes widened and she said more loudly, '*How much for what?*'

At this stage the sensible course for Bruce would have been to excuse himself and leave quickly; but the truth still hadn't dawned on him and he thought he hadn't made himself sufficiently clear. Suspecting that the girl was foreign, he decided to speak slowly and very loudly, as one does when speaking English abroad. He also began to stammer slightly, '*H-how – m-much – for – s-sex?*' he asked. The question was now clear, unambiguous and could be heard by all in the immediate vicinity. The girl's face flushed bright red with anger.

'*What* did you say?' Finally, the dreadful truth dawned on Bruce. Realising his error and observing the now fast-approaching boyfriend who had been just within earshot, he looked round, only to see me rapidly disappearing down the street. He waited no longer but raced after me, showing a remarkable turn of speed for someone with nearly a gallon of beer on board.

I halted just beyond the street corner and collapsed, convulsed with laughter. Initially, Bruce completely failed to recognise the humour in the situation and was quick to voice his personal opinion of my behaviour.

'You b-bastard! You absolute *b-bastard!* You *knew* she wasn't a p-prostitute, didn't you?' After putting another street or two between us, and well away from the increasingly angry boyfriend – who seemed a trifle upset that his girlfriend had been mistaken for a lady of easy virtue – we both sat down on the pavement and howled with laughter until the tears ran down our faces.

This trifling setback didn't dampen our spirits nor reduce Bruce's curiosity and we set off again on our quest. On the next block was the entrance to a club. Here a bouncer was standing at the head of some metal steps leading down to an open cellar door from which emanated a dull light and some music.

'How much to get in?' asked Bruce of the man.

'Ten shillings, mate,' came the reply. We explained that we couldn't afford it.

'Well, you could try the club around the corner. It's cheaper. Just turn left there,' he said, pointing towards the street end. We thanked him and followed his directions to a similar gate and stairway leading into the same building. This entrance was unattended and so without hesitation we scrambled down the steps to find ourselves in a dimly-lit basement. Once inside it was apparent that both entrances led to the same room and when our eyes had grown accustomed to the gloom we headed for the bar.

'Two pints of bitter, please.' It was my round and I addressed this request to a short, perfumed, very camp character behind the bar.

'Waitreth service only,' he lisped, waving limply toward a table, and with a shake of his hair minced to the other end of the bar to talk to his body-building, fake-tanned friend. Bruce and I sat down at the vacant table and within seconds two girls appeared from nowhere and sat opposite us. They were pretty – or appeared so in the subdued light – and asked us if we would like to buy them a drink. Bruce, ever the gentleman, said, 'Yes, of c-course. W-What would you like?' He asked this of the girl nearest him. 'Champagne,' she said without hesitation. I followed suit and asked her friend what she would like, hoping naïvely that she might opt for a Coke or perhaps a small orange juice. 'Champagne,' she declared, with similar promptitude.

Our camp barman came over to take the order and between us Bruce and I just managed to scrape together enough cash to buy a bottle of the fizzy water they called champagne. It was only too apparent to our hostesses that we had run out of money and when the bottle was finished they departed with a brief, 'Thanks for the drink, boys.' Our hostesses having left and with no money for another bottle, the barman's boyfriend invited us to leave – an invitation it was clearly unwise to refuse. And so for the second time that night we found ourselves out on the street.

With little money left, there was no alternative but to start the long walk home. We headed towards Chinatown, and while traversing the outskirts of Soho, we passed an open doorway with a red light visible in the small hallway beyond. Bruce was still keen for one final attempt to find out how much sex cost, so we timidly entered the brothel. After some initial hesitation, Bruce boldly walked up to a little bar, behind which sat a lady who was looking quite uninterestedly in our direction. Looking further into the darkened room I could see a girl dressed as a French tart with her clinging hooped dress and blue beret. She gave me a disdainful look, tossed her head and turned away to talk to another girl who was dressed as a waitress in a short frilly black skirt and a white apron, beneath which her suspenders were prominently visible.

By now Bruce was in no mood to beat about the bush and so came straight to the point. 'H-how much does it cost?' he asked the lady behind the bar.

'Depends what you want,' came the unsmiling response.

This was growing somewhat complicated and, with his usually sharp intellect dulled by the evening's alcoholic beverages, Bruce decided to take a more direct approach. He delved into his pockets and put all the loose change he could find on the bar, while I followed suit.

'W-well, what can we get for that?' he asked.

Back outside on the street once more, Bruce expressed his disappointment that he still didn't know how much sex would cost. 'She might at least have told us before throwing us out,' he moaned.

'Yes, but we *do* know it's more than three pounds sixty five,' I said then added, 'she could have given us our money back. We'll have to walk all the way home now.'

And so we did.

The following week I was attending the Lambeth Hospital where I was learning obstetrics and was on call for the delivery suite. Walking down the corridor in the early hours of the morning in readiness to deliver a baby, I glimpsed a nurse walking towards me. There was something vaguely familiar about her and as she drew closer I realised that this was the girl for whom I had bought champagne the previous Friday night. She looked older than I remembered, but there was no doubting who it was. I offered a smile but as our eyes briefly met she looked down at the floor and hurried past.

* * *

I was now well into my final year as a medical student and my financial situation continued to be a cause for concern. In the past, during times of fiscal crisis, I would have signed on as a labourer on the building site adjacent to the hospital, but now I couldn't risk taking more time out from my studies and memories of the failed pathology exam were still fresh in my mind. Accordingly I attempted a number of different income-generating schemes.

For the princely sum of fifteen pounds, I offered my body up for medical research. The project I agreed to take part in required me to live on a low salt diet for about a fortnight before giving some samples of blood and urine. The diet was ghastly and – worst of all – beer was banned since it contains a significant amount of salt. I stuck to the diet religiously for a whole week and a half but then one Friday evening, I stupidly went to the bar to meet William.

'Haven't seen you for a while, squire. The usual?' asked Ron as he started to pull a pint.

In retrospect, what I should have said was, 'No thanks, Ron, I'm on this salt-free diet. No beer for *me* tonight, thank you very much.' But I didn't. After the briefest of hesitations, I replied 'Yes, please, Ron. Anyone else want one? I hadn't had a beer for nearly two weeks and this opened the flood-gates. I lost all control and had drunk about four or five pints when I began to feel decidedly unwell. I went home and straight to bed, only to wake up the next day with the worst headache I had ever experienced. I presumed this was something to do with the diet and my low salt status. I craved for salt and was greatly relieved when, three days later, the experiment finished and I collected my fifteen pounds – most of which I spent in the bar that evening.

I contemplated playing the piano in pubs, but the theme from the Warsaw Concerto hardly amounted to a comprehensive repertoire. Luckily, a brilliant PUBAR money-making scheme was hatched after an evening's drinking in the nearby Mason's Arms. The Smithfield Market incident was fondly remembered and we thought that if only we had sold the offal we might have made some decent money. The answer was obvious (or so it seemed at the time). We would adopt the offal business model and apply it to fish. All we had to do was to keep drinking until Billingsgate Market opened at five o'clock in the morning; then we would pretend to be *bona fide* traders, buy industrial quantities of fish at trade prices, and sell it on at a profit. Nothing could possibly go wrong.

In the event we bought a stone of kippers. This constituted one crate, amounting to about a hundred fish. Back at Lambeth, we put our entrepreneurial skills to the test and set up a kipper stall outside St Thomas' House. This had been a considerable investment and we were therefore looking for an appropriate return. By lunchtime, however, we had sold only three kippers. Sadly, the kipper market was not as vibrant as our market research – which had comprised asking the people at the next table in the Mason's Arms if they liked kippers – had indicated. Consequently, we ate kippers for breakfast, lunch and dinner for two whole weeks until they were all consumed, and meanwhile PUBAR smelt like a gannetry.

I remained desperate to earn some money and sought inspiration from numerous acquaintances. I heard a rumour that one of the students in the year below, a man known only as George, was about to donate sperm and that this was a nice little earner. Accordingly, I sought him out to ask what was entailed.

'Well, first you have to register with an agency. They will ask you to complete a form with all your characteristics. They tend to like medical students, as they're popular with recipients. They also need to know such things as your hobbies and your physical details. You'll score well, as they like tall people. And you're musical, which is good. You're not Jewish, are you?' I shook my head. 'Shame. That would have ticked all the boxes.'

A few weeks later I asked George how he had fared with his donation. 'Well,' he explained, 'they put you in a little cubicle with some magazines and a container, you know, to do the business. Unfortunately, I missed the pot, but I scraped it off the floor, handed it in and received my twelve quid. You should try it.'

I decided not to.

'Have you tried night-nursing?' asked Simon one evening when we were having a pint in Ron's. I've been doing one night a week at Bart's and it pays well.'

'Tell me more,' I asked eagerly.

Medical students were taken on at St Bartholomew's Hospital as auxiliary nurses on an *ad hoc* basis. My original plan had been to work Friday, Saturday and Sunday nights, while attending lectures as usual from Monday to Friday. There were, however, two problems. The first was that I found it impossible to stay awake at night, while I was expected to be nursing; and the second was that I kept falling asleep during the daytime, when I was supposed to be studying. Apart from those drawbacks, it was a brilliant scheme. I cut back the nursing to two nights a week and persevered long enough to restore my financial situation from dire to just downright bad.

PUBAR was now breaking up. St John and William decided to move into St Thomas' House in the run-up to the finals. I rented a room in a nearby house where my friend Smithie was already ensconced and he helped me move in. This was quite simple as I had few belongings, apart from the piano. With difficulty we manhandled it down the stairs and on to the pavement, during which exercise the dampers once again became detached from the mechanism. We then had to cross Queenstown Road. It was about six o'clock in the evening and in retrospect the rush hour was probably not an ideal time for this undertaking. We waited for a gap in the traffic and then, with a, 'Right now, *quick*,' from Smithie, pushed the piano as hard and as fast as possible across the road. Not all the drivers were as courteous as they might have been, but we eventually made it across without causing an accident. As we rested, sweating and breathless on the other side of the road while leaning on the piano, a car pulled up alongside us. The driver wound down his window and, pointing toward Chelsea Bridge, called out, 'The Albert Hall's that way, mate.' How we laughed.

My new flat was only fifty yards down the road, but by the time we had dragged and pushed the unwieldy instrument that far we were exhausted and thirsty. Luckily there was a vacant parking space of just the right length immediately outside the flat. We thus abandoned my fine pianoforte at the side of the street between two parked cars and walked to The Pavilion for sustenance. We returned after several pints and a game of darts when, refreshed by the beers, we hauled it up a flight of stairs to my new room and what would prove to be my final residence as a student in London.

* * *

The young athletic-looking registrar suddenly halted mid-stride. He had been walking rapidly along the hospital corridor and this was so unexpected that those of us following him bumped into each other, almost knocking him over. This was a pre-finals teaching round, an attempt to hone our clinical skills for the forthcoming exams with a series of rapid-fire questions and answers.

'You!' He looked at William. 'What do you think that abdominal mass was?'

'I think it could be a pancreatic pseudo-cyst.' As always William spoke slowly, but now as he enumerated his reasons for this diagnosis, there was a confidence and authority in his manner that had not previously been present. There had been a subtle change in his whole demeanour which was difficult to define. Certainly he now *looked* professional. Gone were the jeans and crumpled clothes. He now sported a tidy haircut, neatly-ironed crisp white shirt, trousers with a crease where it ought to be, and polished black brogues. Sartorially he looked more like the schoolboy I had met five years earlier, but now his whole bearing was that of a caring, responsible young doctor. I looked at the rest of our group. To differing degrees, we had all undergone a transformation: a gradual evolution, not just in appearance, but also in our attitude to colleagues and the populace at large – our future patients. Unwittingly and unknowingly we had been transformed from irresponsible schoolboys, through untidy, irreverent students to burgeoning doctors. Somewhere along the line we had changed, and now we had more than just a veneer of respectability and knowledge.

'What are the five 'F's?' our tutor continued.

'Causes of abdominal distension,' someone shouted from the back of the group.

'Right. I want one 'F' from each of you. *You* first,' our tutor continued, pointing at me. 'Flatus,' I said. His pointing finger quickly moved to Arthur standing next to me. 'Fat.' Then it was St John's turn. 'Faeces,' he said.

'Yes. Next.'

'Fluid.' This was Simon's response.

'Right. Last one.' It was Mike's turn. He looked up for inspiration, then down at his feet. No answer was forthcoming. 'Anyone?' asked our teacher.

'*Foetus*,' the rest of us chorused.

'Yes, remember! Any female between the ages of fifteen and fifty is pregnant till proved otherwise. You would do well to remember that. Now, let's move on.'

CHAPTER 15:

HAVING A BALL

The Summer Ball was the main social event in the St Thomas' Hospital student calendar. At a certain date in late May the sports ground at Cobham would be converted into a spectacular venue: part funfair, part dance hall, part pop festival – and many parts pub. At around twenty pounds a ticket it was costly and for many years I felt I couldn't possibly justify the expense, but in my last summer as a medical student Smithie and I decided to treat our girlfriends and ourselves to this extravaganza. We also persuaded our old chums from Norwich, Bruce and Frank, to join our party.

Bruce had a car – not just any car but a Citroën 2 CV, a deux-chevaux, or flying dustbin. Known by many epithets – none very complimentary – those cars, rarely seen now, were fascinating vehicles, a form of missing link between four-legged transport and proper cars. Their distinguishing features included: a bonnet which resembled a dustbin lid, a roof which consisted of a canvas strip which invariably leaked when it rained but could be rolled back when the weather was fine, seats which were essentially deck-chairs, and windows which inexplicably opened outwards and upwards rather than in the more traditional downwards direction.

The main problem for the driver, however, was not related to any of those idiosyncrasies but to the mechanism for changing gear, which must have proved a complete mystery to all but the French. In contrast to the more usual gear lever projecting from the floor, this one protruded from the dashboard and resembled a short walking stick. I had driven Bruce's car on a number of occasions and judged there seemed little rhyme or reason for engaging any particular gear. My driving technique was to press the clutch pedal as far down as it would go, grasp the stick firmly in my left hand and manipulate it vigorously, while at the same time twisting a little handle on the end. If this were done for long enough, eventually there would follow a crunching sound and that was the sign to let in the clutch very, very carefully and then wait to see what occurred. As there was no way of knowing exactly which gear had been engaged, the result was entirely unpredictable and both driver and passengers would usually find themselves thrown forward or backward in a completely random fashion. I still believe that this gear-stick mechanism is the reason why the French drive like maniacs.

As well as being fair-weather only cars, the other well-known feature of 2CVs was their inherent instability. At any speed in excess of ten miles an hour it was essential for both driver and passengers to lean into a corner to avoid the risk of the car overturning. Negotiating a turn was thus rather like tacking a yacht in high winds. Regular passengers knew the drill and, if Bruce (or 'skipper', as the driver of a 2 CV was usually known) wished to change direction significantly, it was implicitly understood that he would need the assistance of his crew. Thus, for an impending left-hand corner, Bruce would shout, 'Going left soon,' then, 'Lean left – *now.*' And, as he spun the steering wheel, we would all lean over as far as space permitted to ensure a smooth change of direction. Apart from those minor design flaws and the fact that with its bonnet open it strongly resembled a feeding stegosaurus, the 2 CV really was an excellent vehicle.

Rose had agreed to accompany me to the ball and Smithie was bringing a friend of hers whom he had met in the aftermath of the little unpleasantness at Gassiott House. On the evening in question and dressed smartly in our dinner suits, the pair of us walked the short distance from our residence to The Pavilion where we were to meet our partners. We arrived early in order to start the evening with a couple of pints and a game of darts, and were well ensconced at the bar when the door opened and Rose entered, accompanied by her friend. The hubbub ceased as everyone's gaze was drawn towards them and there came a low whistle from the far end of the room. Both girls looked quite stunning in their long ball gowns, delicate make-up and dangling jewellery. Rose had changed little in her appearance over the years since I had first met her. With her bobbed hair, pretty snub-nosed face and decidedly plummy accent, she remained the epitome of a well-brought-up public school girl. I recalled with considerable nostalgia the first night I had met her at that smoky party in Clapham three years before. Tonight she looked ravishing. Not someone who habitually wore make-up, she now displayed luscious deep-red lips, dark enticing eyes, while the blackness of her low-cut evening gown bestowed a seductive allure. Even The Pavilion's most ardent regulars would not have called it an elegant or sophisticated pub. It was more a beer and pie stall than a champagne and oyster establishment, and consequently its clientele were wholly unaccustomed to such elegance. After a brief silence as the girls entered, the regulars deferentially stood back to let Rose and her friend approach the bar where Smithie and I were stationed.

'Gosh! Rose, you look wonderful,' I said, looking her in the eyes while grasping both her hands.

Her face lit up with a bright smile of delight. 'You needn't sound so surprised, Grahame.' She looked me up and down, 'You look pretty good yourself!' Then after a pause she added, 'I'll have a gin and tonic, please.' By the time our drinks arrived, the noise and conversation in the pub had returned to normal and shortly afterwards Bruce arrived with his partner, followed by Frank, who had driven down from Norwich specially for the occasion. Frank was alone being (in his own words) 'between girlfriends', but declared that he was entirely confident of meeting someone at the ball for company and (as the singles adverts say) 'possibly more'. Frank had a proper car, a souped-up Ford Escort which came equipped with a large exhaust, made a growling sound and travelled at rather more than twenty-five miles an hour.

After introductions had been exchanged and with our drinks finished, we set off on the forty-five minute drive to Cobham. As the evening was fine and it didn't look likely to rain, Rose and I decided it was safe enough to travel with Bruce and his girlfriend in the 2 CV. Smithie, along with his partner for the evening, settled into the Escort and with Frank at the wheel they roared off in the direction of Cobham with us trailing ever further behind. As Frank's car rapidly disappeared into the distance, the flying dustbin's speedometer resolutely hovered at twenty-one miles an hour.

'Steady on, Bruce!' I said, glancing across at our driver. 'Are you trying to get us arrested for speeding?' I laughed as Bruce looked at his speedometer.

'D'you want us to go a bit faster?' he asked.

It was Rose who replied in all seriousness, 'That would be good if possible, Bruce, as it would be nice to get there sometime tonight.' She had calculated that at our current speed we wouldn't arrive till the early hours of the following day.

'Okay, hold on to your seats.' Bruce then leant forward and gave the speedometer a sharp tap with the forefinger of his left hand. The needle shot up to an impressive thirty-five miles an hour. 'Ah, that's better,' he said, and smiled as he eased himself back into the deckchair that he called a driving seat.

The pavilion and sports ground at Cobham had been utterly transformed. The sun was setting when we arrived and the bright twinkling lights of a helter-skelter greeted us at the entrance. Nearby, a siren wailed to announce the start of the Dodgem ride, whereupon black-tied drivers, with their gowned co-drivers set about chasing each other around the shiny metal track. Three enormous marquees stood all in white against the green backdrop of the rugby pitches. It was a fine, balmy night and a glorious cacophony of musical styles filtered from the tents, coupled with a confused, but enticing, smell of hot doughnuts and fried onions. In the reddening evening sun, beautiful young women in flowing dresses, and handsome men with satin lapels, frilly shirts and black bow-ties, sauntered through the fairground attractions. They clutched flutes of champagne or pints of beer, while laughing loudly and flirting openly. I showed Frank around, introduced him to a few of my friends and left him in a group at one of the numerous bars, drinking beer and trying to seduce the barmaid.

Rose and I held hands and, wandering between marquees, from the bright noise of the steel band to the dark silence of the moonlit pitches, we drank, ate, danced and kissed our way through the night. In the dim light of the emerging dawn, I spotted the distinctive figure of William silhouetted against one of the marquees with his arm around Jane's waist. I slapped him hard on the back causing him to spill his beer. Annoyed, he turned around angrily before his expression melted into a wide smile of recognition. 'Hello, Grahame. Hello, Rose. Having a good time?'

We were standing in the glare of arc lamps which lit the entrance to the Helter-Skelter. William directed his gaze towards the apex of its brightly-painted tower and after a brief pause asked, 'Hey, Grahame, do you think you could slide all the way down carrying a full pint, without spilling a drop, and then sink it in one at the bottom?' Even at this stage of the night he still spoke in his customary slow and precise tones.

Rose looked at me disapprovingly, and then glanced at Jane who responded with a similar grimace. 'Easy!' I said. '*You're on.*' We bought fresh pints, clambered to the top and there, once carefully seated on coconut mats, we sped down, showering beer over ourselves and those below, before tumbling to the ground from where we rose unsteadily to our feet and laughingly drank what was left. Other revellers attempted to walk along the ridge of the tents, only to slip and slide down on their backsides. Many beers and much champagne was drunk. The girls were all beautiful and the men handsome; we were young, privileged and, for a brief moment in time, had not a care in the world.

In such a large crowd it was easy to lose touch with others, but half-way through the evening I realised that I hadn't seen Frank for quite some time. However, I was having a good time and didn't bother to search him out. Far too soon the sky grew lighter, the sun came up and we began to seek out our friends with the prospect of heading home. I soon found Bruce, who was happy to drive the flying dustbin once again, but there was no sign of Frank. We searched the marquees without success and had all but given up when I decided it would be wise to relieve myself before embarking on the journey home and so went to the nearest toilet, which was in the changing-rooms. There, curled up on a slatted wooden bench, lay Frank – fast asleep. He had left the girl I had seen him with to visit the Gents and had then decided to take a little rest. There he had dozed off at about ten o'clock and thereafter slept soundly all night.

I started to rouse him. 'Frank,' I said, gently nudging his shoulder. 'Frank, it's me, Grahame. Time to go home.' It was the Star of India all over again, but how were we to convince him he had enjoyed a long night of dancing and philandering when in fact he had slept through it all?

'Right! Thanks,' he said. 'Must've dropped off for a moment. Anyone for a beer?' We broke it to him gently that it was five in the morning, the ball was over and it was time to go home.

'You peaked too early.' I said.

'Oh, *no!*' He stared at his watch in the hope that I was joking, but the truth slowly dawned on him that he had missed the whole event. 'You might at least have woken me,' he complained.

'No one knew where you were,' I explained.

Frank blearily began to review the situation and then started to chuckle. 'At least I'm fit to drive, which is more than can be said for most of you.' He straightened his black bow-tie and set off in search of any attractive girls who might be in need of a lift back to London – and 'possibly more'!

Rose and I wandered back to the flying dustbin and squeezed into the back while Bruce, with his girlfriend in the passenger seat, set about firing up the engine. After several failed attempts, Bruce finally engaged a forward gear and we set off for St Thomas' where we were to drop Rose off for a late shift that afternoon. It was a fine morning and with the canvas roof rolled back, a pint mug full of beer in my hand and Rose at my side, life could not have felt better. In fact it seemed so good that, as we were driving along the Albert Embankment and approaching St Thomas', I decided to stand bolt upright so that the full length of my torso extended through the open roof of the car. There, my arms outstretched with a pint-mug in one hand, I began to serenade Rose with – appropriately I thought – Verdi's *Nessum Dorma,* while toasting bemused early bird pedestrians. Bruce encouraged me to sit down, complaining that the car was becoming difficult to handle since its centre of gravity had risen by a foot or two. I took this as an open invitation to sing yet more loudly, and the flying dustbin consequently began to sway dangerously. I cannot now be sure who spied the police car first but Bruce yelled, 'Sit down!' just as I saw the car overtaking us, its blue light flashing. I sat down quickly

'Oh, shit! That's it,' said Bruce. 'I'm well over the limit.'

Bruce pulled over as requested and parked behind the police car. Two policemen got out and strolled slowly towards us. Bruce opened the window flap upwards and, as the officers drew close, said brightly to the nearest one, 'Good morning, officer,' in a casual style that implied that he could not for the life of him think of any reason why the police should have pulled us over. He gave the impression that it was perfectly normal to be driving a 2 CV while wearing a dishevelled dinner suit, accompanied by three passengers, one of whom had been standing up through the roof toasting passers-by with an empty pint mug and singing *Nessum Dorma* at the top of his voice.

'Had a good night, lads?' the nearest policeman asked. This was really a rhetorical question by way of introduction, and was code for – 'Okay, so you're pissed up after a party, you're behaving like idiots and what are we going to do with you?'

Bruce, however, felt that a response was required. 'Yes. Excellent, thanks very much.' And then in a moment of utter madness added, 'and have you had a successful night, gentlemen of the constabulary?' The policeman clearly didn't think it necessary to respond to this polite enquiry.

'Where have you been?' enquired the officer. We explained that we were medical students heading back to St Thomas' after the Summer Ball. As we were making our excuses and contritely apologising for our behaviour, the radio in the police car crackled into life and one of officers went to respond. On his return the two policemen muttered briefly to each other and then one of them walked briskly over. 'Are you *definitely* going back to St Thomas'?' he asked brusquely, looking along the road to where the hospital was just visible about a mile away. We reassured him that was the case.

'Well, go straight there and *nowhere* else.' Then he added, 'And *don't* stand up. You know how unstable these cars are at the best of times.' Turning around, he raced back to the police car which set off at speed, its siren screeching and blue light flashing.

As it disappeared along the Embankment we breathed a collective sigh of relief.

'Jesus! That was a bit of luck.' We all agreed with skipper Bruce who then, after a great deal of grinding and crunching, eventually found a forward gear and drove us the short distance back to the hospital.

We later calculated that, for the amount of money we had spent on attending the ball, we could have had a package holiday in Spain for a week, but most of us felt that the experience had been well worth it. Not so, however, Frank, who remained peeved that, once again, he had peaked too early.

Finals were now only weeks away and we were all acutely aware that it was essential for us to study as hard as possible in order to pass this ultimate hurdle. Revision was largely a matter of imbibing, not beer but, huge amounts of information and regurgitating it to order. I could do this relatively easily if I put in long hours, but knowledge and understanding are quite different attainments and using this information in a clinical setting as a junior doctor was to prove a major problem for me in the future. Meantime, I virtually memorised several large texts and rehearsed answers to all the questions I could possibly think of. My method was to sit at a desk for eight or ten hours a day, making list upon list, sticking them to the walls of my room with Blu Tack and reciting them over and over until they were imprinted upon my cerebral cortex.

Simon, on the other hand, had discovered that he revised best when sitting on the floor of a paternoster. I had never before, or indeed have never since, seen a paternoster lift but there was one in a stairwell just off the main corridor of the hospital. Here a continuous chain of linked cubicles, attached to a kind of giant bicycle chain, travelled up and down from the basement to the top floor. At the top and bottom of its travel there was a noisy cross over as the cubicle changed direction. There were no doors and one simply stepped on and off at will. There was a notice in each cubicle requesting that occupants should alight at the top and the bottom. Simon ignored this and would frequently be seen, text in hand, sitting on the floor of the paternoster ascending and descending for hours on end. Sometimes he would be reading, sometimes talking to other occupants of the lift and sometimes lying propped up in the corner, sound asleep.

Apart from revision tutorials, there was little formal teaching at this stage. As well as learning large tracts of our textbooks by rote, we refined our clinical skills and examination techniques in as many ways as possible – which for many of us involved persuading our girlfriends to let us practice on them on a regular basis. Less pleasurable, but equally essential, was the business of endlessly patrolling the wards to inspect exotic rashes, identify curious heart sounds and to palpate peculiar lumps and bumps. I discovered one old man who had managed to survive the Western

Front only to develop trench foot living rough in Lambeth and all such interesting finds were shared with our colleagues.

'Wonderful aortic stenosis on Florence Ward, bed six, just on the left.' This came from Charles who was standing behind me in the lunch queue. 'The murmur's so loud you can actually hear it from the end of the bed!'

'Thanks, Charles. You might like to check out the abdomen of the old guy – second on the right, Cheselden Ward, bed twenty-two. Lovely aneurysm. You can't possibly miss it.' Then I added, 'You'd better be quick though. He didn't look too well when I last saw him.'

'Thanks, Grahame.' And Charles raced off without waiting for his lunch.

One of the last things we were taught, perhaps appropriately enough, was how to certify death. That skill, you may imagine, should be relatively easy, but the exact moment of death can prove very difficult to define. Muscles twitch and corpses may appear to take breaths *post mortem*, while electrical activity on an electrocardiograph may persist for hours. Conversely, some patients who appear to have shuffled off this mortal coil, may show signs of life once more, albeit only for a short time. Over subsequent years I have been premature in diagnosing death on at least one occasion.

Arthur set about his revision as he did everything else – he wrote numerous timetables. He spent so much time writing those that it left little opportunity for actual revision. One night, all the old PUBAR residents were having a beer in Ron's when William observed, 'D'you know, chaps, every time we get inebriated we lose a few million neurones?'

'Bloody hell! Is that right?' queried St John, 'I need every last neurone that I can muster just now.' We all agreed, so most of us stopped drinking or at least dramatically reduced our alcohol intake and needless to say bar profits plummeted. After his first week of abstention St John proudly announced that he had passed his first solid stool for five years.

And thus we headed towards a series of exams spanning almost two months, which, if we passed, would mean that we might actually call ourselves doctors.

CHAPTER 16:

THE END OF AN ERA

The summer of 1976 was dominated by our final exams. These were spread over a protracted and stressful period of several weeks. The classroom subjects, Pathology and Pharmacology, had been examined in the spring and everyone had passed. That left the less predictable subjects of Medicine, Surgery, Obstetrics and Gynaecology. All of those involved a written paper, followed by an oral and a clinical exam, the last of which involved taking a history and examining patients. Most of us had spent hours memorising textbooks, while Simon, when he wasn't in the paternoster, was known to sit at his desk staring fixedly at a postcard on the wall, picturing a student seated at *his* desk gazing out of his window. It carried the caption: 'One day I will start to enjoy myself'. It constantly reminded me of that surrealist picture where a man in a bowler hat is looking into a mirror at an image of the back of his own head.

We sat the written papers at examination halls in Queen's Square, a region I had only previously frequented for its selection of excellent pubs. Those included The Queen's Larder, which had been a favourite haunt when we had been in halls of residence nearby. Unfortunately our intimate knowledge of the local hostelries was not to prove of significant help in the exams – as Arthur was soon to learn. After the Surgery written paper he was disconsolate and as we walked out of the examination hall he declared pessimistically, 'Well! That's it! I've failed. There's no *way* I could possibly have passed that exam.'

'Why not?'

'I just *know*.' He fingered his telescopic umbrella restlessly, and then, after looking skyward at the beautiful cloudless day, reluctantly replaced it in his briefcase.

'Arthur, I'm sure you'll pass. Why d'you think you've done so badly?' I tried to press him, but he wouldn't be drawn. He looked up at the heavens again, as though willing it to rain so that he could conceal his misery beneath the canopy of his umbrella, but the sky remained resolutely clear and sunny.

'The only good thing that's going to happen to me this year,' he continued, 'is my wedding in December.' Arthur had proposed to Jess and been accepted. When St John heard this he felt that some of the credit for this successful wooing should belong to him, in consequence of his intensive nocturnal serenading in the early stages of that courtship. For myself, I was particularly pleased with the written exam in General Medicine and felt that I should have at least scraped a pass in the others.

Both the *viva voce* and clinical exams involved appearing in front of the examiners. 'If you don't wear a suit you'll fail,' warned one of our tutors. He then explained that in a previous year one student had turned up in a houndstooth sports jacket. The examiner had advised the student to change into a suit before the next exam session in the afternoon or else he would be failed – and had even phoned ahead to ensure the student had done so. I still didn't have a suit and wore the same combination of almost matching charcoal-grey jacket and trousers that I'd worn for my interview nearly six years before. My General Medicine clinical exam was to be at the Royal Free Hospital in Hampstead, a part of London I had never explored, while Obstetrics was at the Middlesex Hospital. In the latter instance I had approximately twenty minutes in which to examine a heavily pregnant lady before being ushered into a room to face a trio of interrogators. I was asked about the history of the pregnancy – which had been uneventful – and my clinical findings. 'How many weeks into the pregnancy is she, do you think?' asked one of my inquisitors. I had measured the fundal height of the uterus (how high the bump is above the pubic bone) and gave my estimate.

'I think she's at about thirty-eight weeks, sir.'

'That's correct. What position do you think the foetus is in?'

'I think it's right occipito-posterior, sir,' I replied.

'Good. And for a full house, is the head engaged?' By now, I knew I was doing well.

'I could feel the head and it was fixed. I am confident that it is engaged, though not yet fully descended into the pelvis.'

'Well done! That's all.' The examiners all looked up and smiled as I headed for the door, confident of having passed.

The results of these exams were published piecemeal over a period of several days. I knew I had passed Surgery along with Obstetrics and Gynaecology but still awaited the results of the General Medicine exam. When they came I was surprised to find I had done well – in fact so well that I had been invited back for an honours viva. This was something of a mixed blessing. To achieve honours in any subject was a significant achievement, but involved yet another *viva voce* about a week later which meant that I couldn't afford to relax and celebrate fully. Nor, indeed, could I summon up the energy or enthusiasm to do more work. I had been so focussed on the end of the exams that suddenly to have one more added was deeply disconcerting.

I received a message that the Professor of Medicine wished to see me – for what I presumed would be a tutorial. We met in Ron's bar and after ordering two half-pints of beer he took me aside. 'Well done,' he said, shaking my hand. 'These honours *vivas* are funny things. They're unique in that you can only *improve* your result, since you've already passed. The best advice,' he continued, 'that I can give you is just to keep your eye on the ball and, if you can, hit it for six.' I nodded, and looked expectantly at him for some more pertinent advice, but he simply said, 'Good luck! Aim for the boundary.' He smiled, shook my hand again and moved to leave. I thanked him for this invaluable guidance and went to celebrate with the others in the bar. On the day of the exam I must have foolishly taken my eye off the ball, since I was clean-bowled, middle-stump, first delivery.

Most of us – including Arthur, to his amazement – had passed all the exams. Unfortunately Charles had failed – badly – and when all the results were finally published, the ex-PUBAR residents met up with him in the bar. He congratulated each of us, and blinked back the tears as we all commiserated with him. However, all was not lost for Charles, as he re-sat the exams later that summer and passed every one with flying colours. When asked how he had managed to turn abject failure into stunning success in such a short period of time, he simply smiled enigmatically and said, 'It's amazing what you can do with a virgin brain.'

Then followed the business of applying for our first posts as doctors. We were required to spend a year as housemen – half each in surgery and medicine – before deciding which branch of medicine we might wish to specialise in. The most prestigious posts were those in one's own teaching hospital and we all therefore applied for one or more. I submitted an application to be houseman on the professorial surgical unit. An element of my reasoning for applying for this particular post was that I hoped the professor in question might recall how I had caught his daughter when she had fainted, almost certainly saving her life, and that this might count in my favour. Sadly, it didn't and I was disappointed not to be offered a house-job at St Thomas'. Upon reflection that may have been hardly surprising in view of the little incident of the stitch-cutting, not to mention my prolonged absenteeism while working on the building site.

William had matured into a promising young doctor. Outwardly he had changed little and still spoke in that slow, deliberate voice that I had first heard nearly six years previously when we met outside the Nevin lecture theatre. Over the years, however, he had acquired an air of authority and self-confidence which was most impressive, and I was not surprised to learn that he had been offered the post of houseman on the medical unit – a plum post at St Thomas'. St John also was offered a teaching hospital post as a surgical houseman. There he developed a lifelong interest in head and neck surgery, but still yearned to improve his musical skills. He applied for a cello course at the Royal School of Music, and when turned down took to playing his instrument on the pavement outside the professorial residence there. Eventually the lady in question succumbed and cajoled one of her senior students into giving him lessons.

The rest of us were appointed to posts in affiliated hospitals outside London. Arthur had changed little over the six years since I had known him. He still wore the same beige raincoat, or at least one very similar, and carried about his person that ever-present telescopic, self-opening umbrella. His confidence had been dashed on a number of occasions over the years, yet he always bounced back, even brighter and more self-assured than before. Arthur's focus was now on his forthcoming wedding and he began preparing for that event in his own inimitable way. He remained pleasantly surprised at having passed his final exams and was delighted to accept a post in a hospital on the south coast. I myself was interviewed and offered the post of surgical houseman at Leicester General Hospital.

There was to be no grand finale to our time as medical students and the summer fizzled out, rather like a damp squib. Even the building site was closed since the new hospital block had now been completed. Queen Elizabeth herself was to open it formally and Bob, our hoist-man and rock'n'roll star, was invited to join the reception party. He spent weeks washing his calloused hands and using moisturising cream in preparation for shaking the monarch's hand. As for us newly-qualified doctors, we all had to wait several months before taking up our posts in February of the following year. Some went home, some started locum posts while Arthur prepared for his wedding by asking me to be his best man.

As for Rose – time, distance and the pressures of being a junior doctor separated us, and so we gradually drifted apart. I still recall her face, however, framed by that bob of chestnut-brown hair, and can hear her infectious giggle; and I will always remember how, over my student years, whenever I was lonely she was always there for me. The last I heard of her she was working for a charity, nursing in the slums of Delhi.

And what of me? I had been exposed to an eclectic cross-section of humankind, both in and out of the medical fraternity. I was still tall and gawky, with a tendency to shyness and a predilection for imbibing too much beer, but I had been exposed to some of the harsher tragedies of life at both a personal and professional level. Like my friends and colleagues, I had evolved and matured during my years at St Thomas' and, although undoubtedly some opportunities had been missed, many had been gratefully and enthusiastically grasped. Before me there now lay the challenge of being a junior hospital doctor – and life could never be quite the same again.

Thus, like an ocean liner slipping its moorings in the calm of the night, with barely a ripple our days as students imperceptibly drifted from the present into the past.